Oil and Chemical Spills

Titles in the Man-Made Disasters series include:

MAN-MADE
DISASTERS

Oil and Chemical Spills

Peter Owens

LUCENT
BOOKS®

THOMSON
—★—™
GALE

San Diego • Detroit • New York • San Francisco • Cleveland • New Haven, Conn. • Waterville, Maine • London • Munich

LIBRARY OF CONGRESS CATALOGING-IN-PUBLICATION DATA

Owens, Peter, 1945-
   Oil and chemical spills / by Peter Owens.
     v. cm. — (Manmade disasters)
Contents: Oil Spills — Deadly chemicals on the loose — The spills of
war — Response and cleanup — Preventing oil and chemical accidents.
   ISBN 1-59018-057-7 (hardcover : alk. paper)
   1. Oil spills—Environmental aspects—Juvenile literature. 2. Chemical spills—Envi-
ronmental aspects—Juvenile literature. [1. Oil spills. 2. Chemical spills. 3. Pollution.]
I. Title. II. Series.
   TD196.P4O94 2004
   628.5'2--dc21
                                                                2003011263

Printed in the United States of America

Contents

Foreword

I n the late 1990s a University of Florida study came to a surprising conclusion. Researchers determined that the local residents they surveyed were more afraid of nuclear accidents, chemical spills, and other man-made disasters than they were of natural disasters such as hurricanes and floods. This finding seemed especially odd given that natural disasters are often much more devastating than man-made disasters, at least in terms of human lives. The collapse of the two World Trade Center towers on September 11, 2001, was among the worst human-caused disasters in recent memory, yet even its horrific death toll of roughly three thousand pales in comparison to, for example, the 1976 earthquake in China that killed an estimated seven hundred thousand people.

How then does one explain people's overarching fear of man-made disasters? One factor mentioned by the Florida researchers related to the widespread perception that natural hazards are "acts of God" that no one can control. Earthquakes, forest fires, and the like are thus accepted as inevitable. Man-made disasters are viewed differently, as unpredictable yet maddeningly preventable. Even worse, because these new technologies are so incredibly complex—a 747 airliner has 6 million parts, the 100-foot-long control room of a nuclear power plant has thousands of gauges and controls—the root cause of the disaster can often be shockingly trivial. One notorious 1972 airliner crash occurred when a tiny lightbulb, the indicator for whether the nose landing gear was down, burned out. While in flight, the captain, copilot, and engineer decided to replace the bulb. With the crew distracted, someone in the cockpit accidentally disengaged the autopilot and the plane flew into the ground, killing 98 of 176 onboard.

Man-made disasters are also distressing because they are so furtive in their deadliness. The hazardous radiation emitted by the nuclear accident at Tokaimura, Japan, in 1999 could neither be seen nor smelled, and the lethal gas that leaked from a Union Carbide pesticide factory in India in 1984 settled silently over the city of Bhopal, killing thousands in their homes.

Another factor may be the widespread perception that man-made disasters are worse than ever. This is probably true although faulty designs and shoddy workmanship have been causing building collapses, dam failures, and ship sinkings for thousands of years. Beginning with the twentieth century, what is new is industrial technology, such as nuclear power and oil refining, that can affect huge areas over many years when something goes wrong. The radiation from the disaster at the Chernobyl nuclear power plant in 1986 spread world-wide and has closed local areas to human habitation to this day. Finally, man-made disasters have begun to compound each other: In January 1997, a massive oil spill caused by the shipwreck of a Russian tanker in the Sea of Japan threatened to clog crucial cooling systems in nearby nuclear power plants.

Fortunately, humanity can learn vital lessons from man-made disasters. Practical insights mean that ocean liners no longer ply the seas, as the *Titanic* did, with too few lifeboats and no ability to see in the dark. Nuclear power plants are not being built with the type of tin-can containment building that Chernobyl had. The latest generation of oil tankers has dou-ble hulls, which should vastly reduce oil spills. On the more philosophical level man-made disasters offer valuable in-sights into issues relating to progress and technology, risk and safety, and government and corporate responsibility.

The Man-Made Disasters series presents a clear and up-to-date overview of such dramatic events as airplane crashes, nuclear accidents, oil and chemical spills, tragedies of space exploration, shipwrecks, and building collapses. Each book in the series serves as both a wide-ranging introduction and a guide to further study. Fully documented primary and secondary source quotes enliven the narrative. Sidebars high-light important events, personalities, and technologies. An-notated bibliographies provide readers with ideas for further research. Finally, the many facts and unforgettable stories re-late the hubris—pride bordering on arrogance—as well as the resiliency of daring pioneers, bold innovators, brave res-cuers, and lucky survivors.

Large-Scale Disasters

Five quarts of oil can lubricate a car engine for five thousand miles against friction and heat, forces that would otherwise destroy an unprotected engine in a trip to the grocery store. The same quantity, barely more than a gallon, can also contaminate 750,000 gallons of water, more than all the water used in a year by two average American families. If that one gallon of oil were multiplied by 68 million, the size of the massive *Amoco Cadiz* oil tanker spill that occurred off the French coast in 1978, the power of oil to cause havoc begins to take focus. It is simply mind-boggling.

Far more potent than oil, a thimble-full of pure liquid chlorine can disinfect hundreds of thousands of gallons of drinking water, killing deadly germs that could sicken hundreds of people. Yet if that chlorine were spilled into a crowded room, it could rapidly evaporate into the air, get inhaled, and be fatal. One company's own risk assessment of its liquid chlorine warned, "In the event of a total failure of a railroad tank car of chlorine which discharges its entire contents within a ten-minute time frame, the resulting cloud of chlorine vapor would be immediately dangerous to both life and health for a distance exceeding fourteen miles."[1] If such an accident occurred in an urban area, thousands of people downwind could be killed or injured.

These are among the trade-offs between progress and disaster that oil and chemicals pose for today's world. When these useful but hazardous substances accidentally spill into the environment, as they often do, they threaten both the natural world and human health.

Potentially Devastating Effects

For the past century the modern world has relied heavily on oil for a variety of purposes. Petroleum is used to make many products that benefit society, from plastics to preservatives. Oil-based plastics make up 80 percent of all toys, 10 percent of car parts, most components in appliances, and even many fabrics. But by far the largest and most important need for oil in modern life is energy, resulting from the enormous worldwide appetite for fuels required in transportation, heat, and production of electricity.

A potent and powerful substance, oil can have devastating effects when accidentally unleashed on the environment. For example, in 1989 the *Exxon Valdez* ran aground in Alaska waters, dumping 11 million gallons of oil into pristine Prince William Sound. Soon after, oil became a weapon of war. Facing defeat in the 1991 Persian Gulf War, retreating Iraqi troops spilled oil from terminals and tankers off the Saudi Arabian and Kuwaiti coasts, a 460-million-gallon disaster, forty times worse than the *Exxon Valdez*. The Iraqis then ignited nearly seven hundred oil wells that belched toxic smoke for nine months and caused illnesses in thousands of people that persist today.

Despite extensive new scientific study and increased government attention, oil disasters have not stopped. In late 2002, the *Prestige* oil tanker spilled 20 million gallons of oil off the coast of Spain, a result of blunders and savage seas. In the past thirty years over ten thousand spills have unleashed billions of gallons of oil into the environment. One element of good news, however, is that the rate of large tanker spills is down by over half from the 1970s, according to industry experts. But shocks such as the *Prestige* continue despite the best efforts of many smart and dedicated people.

The Chemical Spill Parallel

Synthetic chemicals likewise have contributed to advances that increase society's food supply, provide cleaner drinking water, conquer deadly diseases, and more. As a result, the world's dependency on chemicals is rising rapidly. The United States, which is the largest chemical producer in the world, now has some fifteen thousand chemical plants

► A cleanup crew on the coast of Spain contends with oil spilled from the *Prestige* in November 2002.

directly employing over 1 million workers. The value of U.S. chemical shipments was more than $450 billion in 2001, making the chemical industry one of the country's largest manufacturing sectors. The National Transportation Safety Board (NTSB) reports that more than 250,000 shipments of regulated hazardous materials enter the U.S. transportation system every day. Worldwide, chemicals represent a $1.5 trillion industry that produces over 1 billion tons of pharmaceutical, agricultural, construction, and other chemicals each year.

Many chemicals are extremely dangerous, however, especially during their manufacturing and transport. Even when the end products are safe, chemicals are first concentrated in their raw, most dangerous forms in chemical plants, then transported, and then stored again prior to the final production process. Each stage in the raw chemical's life cycle poses opportunities for accidents, and because many chemicals are explosive, unstable, or highly toxic, accidents amid huge bulk quantities can turn quickly into disasters.

Chemical spills can be far deadlier than oil spills and pose even more dire problems at every stage of response. In December 1984, at a chemical plant in the city of Bhopal, India, twelve thousand gallons of methyl isocyanate, a pesticide ingredient, began boiling out of control. That volume of oil would qualify as a minor spill at best. But in its raw state this highly unstable chemical needed to be cooled merely to be stored. When the cooling system failed, the volatile fluid burst into the air like steam over a superheated flame. The Bhopal spill killed thousands of people within minutes from acute poisoning, and twenty thousand died over the next months and years. Today, according to the U.S. Chemical Safety and Hazard Investigation Board (CSB), an independent federal agency, upwards of fifty thousand people remained partially or totally disabled resulting from chronic effects of the disaster.

Unfortunately, chemical disasters like Bhopal have joined oil spills as a worldwide concern. The common thread: The technological underpinnings of life in the industrialized world are growing in size and scope, with ever-larger tankers plying the seas and more massive chemical plants producing increasingly toxic pesticides and other substances. According to a congressional report, 123 chemical plants in the United States each put at least 1 million Americans at risk of exposure to a toxic cloud in the event of a spill or terror event.

An Ongoing Challenge

This book attempts to understand oil and chemical spills in a broad context but largely focuses on dramatic accidents and sudden traumas—highly concentrated events that are often

▲ The December 1984 chemical spill in Bhopal, India, left many of those who survived with serious injuries.

preventable, have specific causes, and unleash common government responses and cleanup strategies. Spills are, however, only a piece of a larger pollution puzzle. They come in many forms, from massive explosions to gradual drips that suddenly burst into public awareness, threatening lethal consequences and long-term effects.

As new petroleum products and synthetic chemicals are developed, manufacturers, government officials, and scientists are struggling against daunting odds to keep a tight lid on them. Regulators at the Environmental Protection Agency (EPA), the United Nations (UN), the European Union (EU), and elsewhere work slowly to improve transportation and production procedures and rules. Their first goal is to prevent spills. When that fails, they turn to improving response time, cleanup techniques, and restoration efforts. With the risk of terrorism in the modern world, plant security poses another expensive and daunting challenge.

Improvements in these areas take time. For example, old single-hull tankers continue to dominate oil shipping, despite new requirements for double hulls on new tankers. All U.S. tankers will be required to have double hulls by 2015, but until then aging fleets remain a problem. Similarly, old railroad cars rust out or jump aging tracks. Pipelines age and rupture. Factories succumb to breakdowns in arcane, immensely complex production processes, and mechanical parts subject to wear fail unpredictably. Terrorism and war pose new, horrific threats, including assaults on these dangerous and fragile technological systems. Unfortunately, the major defenses against spills, including security, prevention, rapid reaction, cleanup, new technologies, and medical treatment, each pose astonishing expenses and enormous complexities that generate bitter political disputes.

CHAPTER ONE

Oil Spills

Modern society is hooked on oil. The United States, the world's biggest oil user, consumes on the order of 250 billion gallons of oil a year. About half of that is imported from foreign countries. Much of the rest travels a long way from northern Alaska, down the Trans-Alaska Pipeline and then by oil tanker to reach refineries and markets.

All of that oil must be extracted from the ground, often in environmentally sensitive areas such as along coastlines. It then must be transported to refineries through pipelines subject to rupture, or by giant tankers vulnerable to storms and shallow channels. The oil is processed and transported again as gasoline and other fuels to every corner of the world. This presents lots of opportunities for various types of accidents and spills on land and at sea, whether due to human error, mechanical malfunctions, or storms.

Awakened by a Blowout

In late January 1969, a drilling rig operating in waters offshore of Santa Barbara, California, unexpectedly hit a pocket of high-pressure oil. The result was a major loss of well control—a blowout—that spewed more than 4 million gallons of crude oil into the ocean for the next three months. As waves washed the oil ashore, it coated more than one hundred miles of Southern California's popular beaches. The violence of the initial blowout opened a fracture in the seafloor underneath the drilling rig, meaning that engineers were helpless to stem the spill for years.

"The nation was suddenly awakened by the Santa Barbara blowout," commented marine conservationist Richard Charter, "to the fact that [offshore] oil and gas technology was not the benign, risk-free operation that the oil industry had led the public to believe. Offshore drilling, it turned out, had a tragic cost and turned out to be prone to accidents that could not be stopped or cleaned up."[2]

A number of reforms and new technologies followed, such as stronger well casings. Government and industry spokespersons gave assurances that such accidents could never happen again. But critics of offshore drilling maintained that the technology was inherently risky. Sure enough, a decade later the *Ixtoc I* exploratory oil rig in the Gulf of Mexico suffered a blowout and caught fire. Before it could be capped and brought under control more than nine months later, the well disgorged almost 150 million gallons of oil that coated much of the Texas coastline. It was one of the worst oil spills in history and killed untold marine life, including thousands of fish and birds. Its cause was, like the Santa Barbara blowout, basically a technical failure.

Diverse Dangers

Since oil can be rapidly dispersed in open water, virtually every oil spill is a frantic race against time. Different methods

▼ The *Ixtoc I* well blowout that began on June 3, 1979, remains one of the worst oil spills in history.

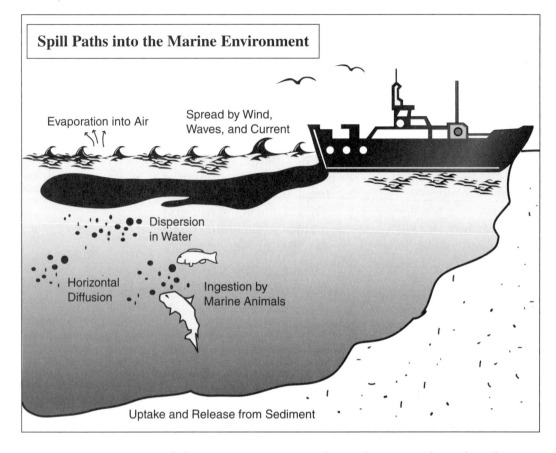

Spill Paths into the Marine Environment

Evaporation into Air

Spread by Wind, Waves, and Current

Dispersion in Water

Horizontal Diffusion

Ingestion by Marine Animals

Uptake and Release from Sediment

of cleanup are necessary depending upon how the oil reacts with water. Refined oil and gasoline evaporate quickly or can be burned off at sea to protect the ocean environment. For example, in January 2003 a tanker off-loading gasoline on Staten Island, New York, blew up, killing two workers. The toxic damage to the nearby environment was minimal compared to a spill of thick, less-volatile crude oil, which forms tarballs and coats marine environments. Most of the gas that did not burn or explode drifted away in currents and evaporated.

Diesel fuel and home heating oil are not nearly as explosive as gasoline but they evaporate more slowly and thus float to more distant shoreline destinations. Along the way they kill fish, birds, and marine mammals. Wildlife that consumes the toxic components of such spills passes the oil poisons into the food chain, eventually reaching humans through consumption of fish or shellfish. So, depending upon the type and level of refinement, oil causes its damage very rapidly or quite gradually, and sometimes both.

Among the most dangerous long-lived compounds of oil are polynuclear aromatic hydrocarbons (PAHs), which can cause cells in the body to mutate, eventually leading to cancer. PAHs have been associated with tumors and deformities in fish and other organisms. Because of the molecular properties of PAHs, they resist weathering and persist in the environment. They are most abundant in crude and heavy oils.

A Critical Blunder

Even when offshore oil is cleanly drilled, there remains plenty of opportunity for disaster as oil tankers confront severe weather or tricky channels and shoals. The sheer number of such barge and tanker trips has increased dramatically in recent years. Accidents at sea happen regularly, and collisions and groundings account for nearly two-thirds of large spills at sea.

Among the most notable examples of a small error in human judgment unleashing major consequences occurred on the night of March 23, 1989, as Captain Joseph Hazelwood guided the *Exxon Valdez* through the waters of Alaska's Prince William Sound. At 11:50 P.M., with only one last hazard, Bligh Reef, to avoid before heading toward open sea, the captain

▼ Workers use high-pressure hoses along Alaska's rocky coast to deal with oil spilled from the *Exxon Valdez*.

inexplicably turned the ship over to third mate Gregory Cousins and left the bridge. He had ordered Cousins to turn a bit to the right at a hazard light near Busby Island, a final move to bring the ship safely into the outgoing shipping lane. Perhaps Hazelwood was a bit weary after having had a few drinks at a local tavern, but he was not drunk and felt Cousins was up to the job.

Cousins began the turn seven minutes too late, and the *Exxon Valdez* ripped into Bligh Reef, tearing a large hole in its hull where oil spewed into the sea. By morning, Prince William Sound and the Gulf of Alaska were stained by huge slicks of shimmering black oil that splashed onto coastal rocks and drenched wildlife. Within days of the *Exxon Valdez* spill, thirteen hundred miles of coastline, equal to the entire eastern coast of the United States, were befouled by gooey black oil. An estimated 250,000 birds died, most from oil saturation.

Hazards Persist Decades Later

Between nature and a massive human cleanup effort, the Alaska coastline began to look nearly normal within a year. But offshore oil spills have now been shown to have long-term adverse effects. As oil weathers over time, it retains its most

NATURE'S FURY

Rules and guidelines can help reduce the likelihood of human error but other factors are not so easily controlled, especially weather. Storms have played a major role in a number of oil spills. Even state-of-the-art, double-hull super tankers are no match for hundred-foot waves in shallow, rocky waters and narrow channels. In December 1976, the 7.7-million-gallon *Argo Merchant* blew eighteen miles off course, in high winds and ten-foot seas, entering an area of treacherous shoals near Cape Cod, Massachusetts. The ship's navigation system failed, and its poorly trained crew was forced to navigate by the stars. As a result it ran aground and spilled its entire cargo of heating oil into the Atlantic. The bad weather that contributed to the disaster saved the shoreline, however, as winds blew most of the floating oil out to sea, where damage was minimized.

This was a ship with a significant and documented history of groundings, collisions, fires, and equipment failures. The *Argo Merchant* had been banned in several ports and denied access to the Panama Canal. Yet it continued to move oil around the world.

stable and dangerous chemical compounds, such as the PAHs that are suspected carcinogens. Marine mammals that ingest spilled oil can suffer kidney failure, nerve damage, and brain disorders. Birds and fish tainted by oil can suffer birth defects and shorter life spans for offspring. New studies of Gulf War soldiers exposed to burned oil over several months in 1991 suggest that the long-term effects of "Gulf War Illness" continue to plague thousands of soldiers more than a decade after their return home.

The evidence is clear. Oil is a dangerous mix of chemicals whose long-term effects are only beginning to be understood. If allowed to persist, oil spills into water, land, and air threaten the fundamental processes of nature that make human survival possible. The Centers for Disease Control considers oil exposure to skin and lungs to be hazardous and capable of causing chronic skin and lung diseases.

Scientists studying the *Exxon Valdez* recently found that toxic hydrocarbon particles that are polluting water at a level as low as a few parts per billion are capable of damaging the

▲ Stormy weather contributed to the grounding of the *Argo Merchant* oil tanker, which spilled its entire cargo as it broke apart and sank.

eggs of pink salmon. Studies by the National Marine Fisheries Service discovered toxins continuing to flow from remnants of *Exxon Valdez* oil more than a decade later. The study said that about twenty-eight beach acres were still contaminated by 15,850 gallons of oil.

In the *Exxon Valdez* aftermath, buried oil has still not yet weathered into a benign state, the fisheries service scientists said. Sea otters and harlequin ducks suffered years later from oil-related stress. Liver samples from otters showed high levels of an oil-related enzyme as a result of eating oil-tainted food and digging in oily beaches. According to a January 2003 news report on studies coordinated by the U.S. Geological Survey, "Sea otters and harlequin ducks in waters near the oil patches still struggled, as recently as last summer, with high death rates and poor reproduction."[3] The populations of

▼ Oil spills often occur in ports, like this 2002 incident involving the North Korean freighter *Chil Song* outside the Japanese city of Hitachi.

birds, fish, otters, and seals were not permanently threatened and have recovered in numbers, but disasters of this magnitude do not simply go away.

Problems at Ports

New regulations put into effect in the United States and worldwide since the spills from the *Exxon Valdez, Argo Merchant,* and other large tankers have attempted to address many of the risks faced by oil-bearing ships at sea. The handling of oil at ports, including loading, storage, and processing, is also heavily regulated. But the recent breakup of the oil tanker *Prestige* illustrates a series of port problems yet to be resolved. *Prestige* was a single-hull vessel so old that it failed European Union port standards and was denied access to Spanish ports. It was forced out to sea, where it broke apart in a storm. Currents spread the huge oil slick over hundreds of miles of Spanish coast.

Oil tankers that run aground in ports pose an immediate threat to coastal waters. In December 2002, a North Korean freighter that ran aground in the Japanese port city of Hitachi spilled crude oil into the water. Other port accidents have involved tankers that caught on fire, as happened to the *Cibro Savannah* at the port in Linden, New Jersey, in March 1990. Some 127,000 gallons of oil were lost into the environment by a combination of spilling and burning. Collisions in the tight confines of ports are another cause of spills, as happened in Tampa Bay in August 1993. Three ships collided and spilled more than 300,000 gallons of fuel oil into the water.

Officials are trying to improve communications to reduce the risk of port spills. Navigation technology has been revolutionized in recent years with global positioning systems, electronic course and map plotters, radar, and precise depth finders. Computerized coordination of these systems adds to safety. Most of this equipment is now inexpensive, and environmentalists contend that today's tanker captains should have no excuse for not knowing where they are. Although technical advances have reduced the number of large spills and shipwrecks, they cannot totally eliminate mechanical failures, nor save a ship from savage seas.

An Oil Tsunami

Oil spills can also take place on land, as a result of leaks or ruptures of pipelines, failure of storage tanks, or accidents during

▶ A March 1993 oil pipeline rupture led to one of America's largest oil spills on land, in Fairfax County, Virginia.

truck or rail transport. Oil spills on land pose many of the same problems as at sea, including the risk of fire and of air pollution from evaporation. Oil can also pollute groundwater.

One of the most dramatic oil spills on land occurred in western Pennsylvania in January 1988, when a 4-million-gallon aboveground storage tank owned by Ashland Oil split. The accident unleashed a thirty-foot wave of diesel oil that swept over a containment dike and across a parking lot. The oil then poured into a storm drain that emptied into the Monongahela River. According to the EPA report:

Within minutes the oil slick moved miles down river, washing over two dam locks and dispersing throughout the width and depth of the river. The oil was carried by the Monongahela River into the Ohio River, temporarily contaminating drinking water sources for an estimated one million people in Pennsylvania, West Virginia, and Ohio, contaminating river ecosystems, killing wildlife, damaging private property, and adversely affecting businesses in the area.[4]

The EPA estimated that only about 20 percent of the oil was recovered during cleanup. Three years later scientists began mapping the badly damaged river to see how and where it was recovering. They released into the water paddlefish, which require good water quality to survive. Most died. It was not until ten years later that paddlefish and other returning species began to thrive in pockets along the river, indicating that the river was improving. The EPA admitted to learning a number of important lessons from this incident, mostly relating to the importance of more rapid, and better coordinated, emergency response.

Difficult Pipes to Inspect

The Ashland Oil tank had been dismantled and moved from an Ohio location. As soon as workers tried to fill it up after it was reassembled at the Pennsylvania facility, it split apart, suggesting that a lack of inspection played a role in the disaster. A different type of land spill occurred when a sixteen-inch-diameter gasoline pipeline in Washington State, owned by the Olympic Pipe Line Company, ruptured in 1999. In less than two hours, 237,000 gallons of gasoline spilled into a creek and ignited, killing three boys, destroying a house, and causing severe damage at a local water treatment plant totaling $45 million. The cause, according to the NTSB, was once again inadequate safety inspections.

Even when oil equipment inspections are done, however, the combination of human error and mechanical failure can lead to accidents. In 1997, workers at a Kentucky facility used internal sensors to inspect a twenty-four-inch oil pipeline. They discovered a dent. Rather than investigate further or excavate to survey the dented pipe, the pipeline company decided to continue operations. Three years later the oil flow was halted for facility maintenance, but the dent had still not

▶ Pipeline spills can be tricky to find and halt, as was this April 1996 underground oil leak on the Trans-Alaska Pipeline.

been investigated or repaired. When the oil flow was restored, the pipeline burst because the dent had weakened the pipe. Over the next three hours, 489,000 gallons of oil poured onto a golf course and into a nearby creek. Low-pressure danger alarms warned of trouble only fifteen minutes after start-up, and had the company shut down then, the spill would have been much smaller.

Human error, faulty inspections, and undetected pipeline damage caused the spill. These are quite typical causes of pipeline spills. But inspecting pipes is not easy. This pipeline was 265 miles long, and a rupture of less than three feet in length led to more than $7 million in environmental cleanup costs. Moreover, pipelines operate at very high pressures. The Kentucky oil line operated at over six hundred pounds per square inch, fifteen times the pressure of an ordinary garden hose. The pipe itself was only one-quarter-inch thick, and at the weak point where the dent had been discovered, the pipe blew open with explosive force.

According to the Environmental Defense Fund, the average pipeline spill in 1998 released over forty-five thousand gallons of oil. Pipeline spills occur frequently enough, moreover, that each year more than 6 million gallons of oil and other hazardous liquids are spilled from pipelines around the world.

An Epidemic of Mini-Spills

Most oil spills are less than two thousand gallons. Between 1974 and 2001, some seventy-eight hundred spills of less than two thousand gallons accounted for more than 90 percent of all spills. The largest category of these small spills happened during loading and discharge operations in port, according to the International Tanker Owners Pollution Federation. Between 1990 and 1999, ten of the largest spills accounted for 75 percent of the oil discharged. But smaller, less catastrophic spills accounted for 25 percent of oil spills, equal to two massive tanker spills.

Small spills add up. In fact, people who change the oil in their cars and then dump the used oil on the ground or down sewers contribute to oil pollution, over the course of a year, equal to a major tanker spill. A similar concern exists on water: One estimate is that accidental oil spills cause only five percent of the earth's water pollution, whereas intentional spills or "operative discharge"—even when

BURIED PROBLEMS

Underground storage tanks are an often-overlooked source of mini-spills, many of which go undetected for years and pollute groundwater. According to a recent survey, as many as 15 million underground tanks store oil and chemicals in the United States. Only about one-tenth of these are regulated, and experts contend that as many as one in four leaks. Unlike major industrial spills confined to specific areas or to predictable transportation routes, these tanks are everywhere and thus pose concerns for homeowners, schools, service stations, and small communities. Cleanup costs often exceed one hundred thousand dollars per spill site, and many environmental scientists say that leaking underground tanks pose one of the country's greatest threats to groundwater, and thus to human health.

▲ Improved technology has helped reduce the number of major spills, such as the 3-million-gallon spill from a Liberian tanker in March 1968 that fouled beaches in San Juan, Puerto Rico.

illegal—represent some 45 percent of that pollution. Plumes from spills out of small, underground storage tanks can spread undetected for many years and pollute wells, yards, houses, and residential neighborhoods. In rural areas, up to 95 percent of drinking water comes from private wells, many vulnerable to these small storage tank spills.

Small spills add up to massive volumes of oil dispersed widely around the planet. They seldom capture headlines and often elude detection for months and even years, sometimes not being discovered until illness in the local population provides the first clues. By then small spills have done much of their damage.

The 100-Million-Gallon Gamble

Factors such as poor planning, human error or carelessness, mechanical breakdowns, and massive storms make it virtually impossible to prevent all oil spill accidents. Technical improvements such as double hulls on tankers may reduce major accidents, and indeed tanker spills exceeding one hundred thousand gallons are down 66 percent since 1990. However, 100 million gallons of oil spill in accidents each year, equal to almost ten *Exxon Valdez* disasters.

To counter these disasters, governments have generated volumes of regulations meant to prevent spills by tightening safety procedures. U.S. government regulations require the oil industry to develop plans to prevent and to clean up spills, and to improve its reporting on spill incidents. Federal law imposes penalties and fines on those responsible for spills. Regulations also assign federal agencies to inspect facilities to ensure compliance, and coordinate spill cleanups. In 1980, Congress enacted the Comprehensive Environmental Response, Compensation, and Liability Act, commonly known as Superfund. It established a tax on the oil and chemical industries so that they now share with the federal government the cost of cleaning up the worst spill sites. In 2002, however, the EPA issued new oil spill rules meant to reduce the regulatory burden on the oil industry. Many environmentalists were critical of the new regulations for softening standards.

A Question of Control

Oil is perhaps the fourth most important product of survival in contemporary human life, exceeded only by air, water, and food. Each of these essential substances is threatened by oil itself. Oil above all is subject to human control, and yet is greatly vulnerable to human error and ignorance. While scientists are making strides in understanding the risks of oil, government and industry alike are struggling to more expertly control this remarkable substance so central to modern life. A similar concern relating to toxic chemicals has become more prevalent in recent years, as more and more industries generate increasing amounts of hazardous materials.

CHAPTER TWO

Deadly Chemicals on the Loose

Modern industries ranging from plastics manufacturing to sewage treatment involve massive volumes of potentially toxic chemicals. U.S. production of hazardous and toxic waste rose from 9 million tons in 1970 to 238 million tons in 1990. Potent chemicals, many much more toxic than oil, are everywhere in the world, with new ones constantly being developed. Dispersed and diluted, most of these chemicals do not represent an acute danger. Yet when circumstances allow them to spill into the environment, they can be an immediate and deadly threat to people and wildlife. The most gruesome example of the catastrophic potential for spilled chemicals occurred in Bhopal. Not only was the immediate toxic effect tragic, but Bhopal illustrates the traumatic lingering effects of chemical exposure. Oil poses enduring effects, as well, but seldom as dangerous to people.

Some of the Culprits

The EPA has four characteristics to consider a substance hazardous: whether it is explosive, can eat or burn through materials ranging from metals to flesh, can mix dangerously with other substances, or is poisonous to living organisms. More than eight hundred substances qualify in one or more of these categories. Some of these, such as pesticides and herbicides, are supposed to be lethal—to insects and weeds. The Bhopal disaster, for example, happened at a pesticide factory. While the targets of pesticides are bugs, the chemical properties that kill bugs are just as deadly to people's cells when unleashed in sufficient volume and concentrations. Those concentrations occur most dramatically during manufacture and transport. Similarly, certain medicines are lethal to germs and safe only when taken in small quantities.

Other potentially toxic chemicals are by-products or ingredients involved in manufacturing otherwise safe products. Solvents, such as those used to clean up certain substances, often contain potent chemicals in highly diluted forms. Chlorine in its safest forms is used to clean clothes and disinfect food handling areas, but it burns skin and eyes and is deadly if swallowed or inhaled. Many household products contain warnings that accidental ingestion may require that consumers induce vomiting and call a physician.

To manufacture many common products, huge undiluted quantities of solvents and other types of chemicals are either created on-site or transported to chemical plants by truck or rail. Chemical production and transport is inherently dangerous. Products such as plastics, for example, require unstable, toxic components while being manufactured. When the final

▼ Bhopal's infamous Union Carbide plant, shown here beyond a shantytown in 1984, used highly toxic chemicals to manufacture pesticides.

product rolls off the assembly line, it is often stable and non-toxic under ordinary conditions. Anything that can separate the original chemical components, however, such as a fire, can release dangerous compounds and once again pose a hazard to living organisms. One simple example is epoxy glue. Two volatile, corrosive, flammable, and toxic chemicals in separate tubes are sold in hardware stores. Mix the chemicals and they react powerfully with each other, giving off toxic gases and heat before solidifying into a relatively harmless, rock-hard substance. But set the solidified substance afire, and its fumes are dangerous again.

With nearly all of these products, there are wastes generated during manufacture. If those wastes spill into the environment, they can raise havoc. So even the most benign baby's rattle is likely to have had a chemical journey through a dangerous stage, and some of the very processes allowing it to become safe for ordinary use were at one point lethal. Such is the remarkable magic and the fascinating Dr.-Jekyll-and-Mr.-Hyde nature of chemical compounds.

A Pickle Jar Spill

Even small chemical spills can be lethal or lead to long-term health consequences such as cancer, birth defects, and a host of gruesome illnesses. In a recent incident, a tiny spill from a mere pickle jar holding eight pounds of liquid mercury was reported as a chemical emergency to the U.S. National Response Center, and the EPA was called in to investigate and coordinate cleanup. One injury was reported, although no mercury was released into the nearby environment. Not all chemicals are as dangerous as mercury, but hundreds are, and thus spills pose a myriad of difficulties.

Spills of liquid mercury are relatively infrequent, but mercury is leaked into the environment through the burning of coal. Likewise, polychlorinated biphenyls (PCBs), toxic compounds used in electrical transformers and other technology, have been culprits in dangerous spills. More commonly, however, PCBs have been released into the environment in the form of waste products once thought to be harmless. Now that PCBs are banned from manufacturing, former waste disposal sites, discarded electrical components, and similar PCB concentrations still pose an environmental threat. Sometimes these are dramatic spills. More often they are the result of rainwater washing through PCB-contaminated soils.

Pesticides similarly enter the environment in large volumes through legal spraying or distribution on farm lands, where they become part of rain runoff, enter streams, or seep into groundwater. Spills at pesticide plants and elsewhere add to an already widespread pesticide presence in the general environment, making assessment of the spill effects more difficult.

Nightmare in India

On a December night in 1984, nearly a million residents of the city of Bhopal in north-central India slept peacefully. Many of them lived in a dreary slum next to the massive Union Carbide pesticide factory. It churned out a new miracle insecticide called Sevin, a supposedly safe replacement for toxic insecticides such as DDT.

One Sevin ingredient, liquid methyl isocyanate, was both deadly and volatile. It required cooling and careful storage. Sensors were installed in the Union Carbide plant to warn of leaks. To save money, however, managers required that

▼ In November 2002 a hospital worker displays a huge photo collage that memorializes some of the thousands who died during the 1984 Bhopal disaster.

refrigerators and sensors be turned off. That night the deadly liquid began to boil in tank number 610, and the pressure from fumes soon burst through a six-inch containment barrier. Technicians in the control room collapsed, coughing and vomiting.

Others not yet exposed ran for water hoses that could dilute the poison and cool the tank, but the tank was too high for the spray to reach. A protective scrubber that could have sprayed a neutralizing soda into the gas failed to work. A safety exhaust stack with a flame that burned escaped gases had also been turned off by managers to save money. The methyl isocyanate gas escaped into the night air over the neighborhood.

World's Deadliest Chemical Disaster

An hour after the leak began, the tank was empty but already thousands of people lay dead or dying, their lungs swollen with fluid, cutting off oxygen to vital organs, drowning them. Others were paralyzed from nerve damage, all of them experiencing horrible pain. Thus began the world's deadliest chemical disaster. The exact toll in lives is not known but Indian authorities estimate that eight thousand people died from acute poisoning within the first few days.

Many people fled to a nearby hospital, where hundreds of victims lay dying in corridors, waiting rooms, and treatment

DEATH ON THE STREETS

"In the fetid, stinking darkness people called for their spouses, children or parents," Dominique Lapierre and Javier Moro write in their recent book *Five Past Midnight in Bhopal*, which details the horror in Bhopal on December 3, 1984. "Then the calling stopped."

> People's throats had constricted from the gas and no one could utter a sound. . . . Stricken by pulmonary edema [fluid-congested lungs], many of them coughed up frothy liquid streaked with blood. Some of the worst affected spewed up reddish streams. With their eyes bulging out of their heads, their nasal membranes perforated, their ears whistling and their cyanotic [purplish, from lack of oxygenated blood] faces dripping sweat, most of them collapsed after a few paces. It was a silent, insidious, and almost discreet massacre. No explosion had shaken the city, no fire set its sky ablaze. Most Bhopalis were sleeping peacefully.

Bhopal was the worst industrial accident in history, Lapierre and Moro note.

suites. Physicians there were uncertain about which chemical they were dealing with and thus had no idea what antidote might work. They were forced to treat people only with water, washing their eyes and faces, forcing terribly sickened people to drink.

Shortly after the deadly cloud escaped, a passenger train pulled into Bhopal station. Hundreds of people disembarked into a deadly cloud. Many rescuers died trying to pull people from homes and streets. Only the next day did pathologists discover the killer chemical, for which there were two common antidotes. By then the damage was done. It was a total breakdown. Everything that could have gone wrong did.

An Ongoing Tragedy

In the years since 1984, there have been as many as twenty thousand Bhopal-related deaths, one hundred and twenty thousand illnesses, and eighty thousand disabilities from chronic effects. A half million people, according to the Indian government, suffered from the effects of the toxic cloud. The Bhopal disaster continues today with up to thirty people dying each month, according to the environmental group Greenpeace. Among the chronic effects Dominique Lapierre and Javier Moro cite are "breathing difficulties, persistent coughs, ulcerations of the cornea, early-onset cataracts, anorexia, recurrent fevers, burning of the skin . . . not to mention constant outbreaks of cancer and tuberculosis."[5]

The cleanup was a dismal failure as well. Samples taken in 1999 by Greenpeace revealed drinking water remained contaminated and was still being consumed by Bhopal residents. Soils near the factory contained dangerous levels of a half dozen additional poisons. Bitter legal disputes prevented the infusion of funds required for restoring such a massive site. Union Carbide fought off hundreds of lawsuits totaling billions of dollars, eventually settling for $470 million, a figure that its critics say is too little and too late to cover the true costs incurred.

What Went Wrong

In recent years a new form of inquiry, based on computer systems analysis, has evolved to study technological disasters.

The common thread of its findings is that single causes are rare. William M. Evan and Mark Manion, university professors and the authors of *Minding the Machines: Preventing Technological Disasters*, identify four elements usually at play: technical design factors, human factors, organizational factors, and sociocultural factors derived from how groups work together.

Each factor may prevent or contribute to a disaster, and each has to be addressed to reduce the chances of new disasters. Surprisingly, technical factors leading to disaster often include attempts to improve old factories, tankers, or railways. Attempts to fine-tune a system, for example, by making it cheaper to run can short-circuit safety systems. Bhopal was fine-tuned that way and was made more dangerous.

Another major factor is failing to build safety margins that protect against human frailty. These human factors include errors of ignorance, whether from an operator making a dumb mistake or from choosing the wrong action due to lack of training or an insufficient understanding of the system. Bhopal included both types of errors of ignorance. Organizational factors include failure to adhere to procedures, rules, standards, and regulations. Bhopal was rife with management lapses, according to Evan and Manion. Failure to adhere to safety precautions became a normal way of doing business that saved money.

Sociocultural factors include acceptance of risk-taking behavior, a lack of value for human life, and indifference to the working conditions of employees. In Bhopal, American managers lacked understanding, compassion, and concern for their Indian employees and the factory neighborhood. To minimize disasters such as Bhopal, all of these system protections need to be in place. In Bhopal none were.

An Accident a Day

Despite a number of notable reforms in the aftermath of Bhopal, as well as increased penalties for negligence, chemical spills at industrial plants have continued in the years since. The U.S. Chemical Safety and Hazard Investigation Board admits that comprehensive and reliable historical records on chemical accidents are lacking, and that many accidents that occur during the production and transportation of chemicals are not reported to the federal government. Various studies within recent years indicate, however, that chemical accidents are common in the United States. An EPA study, for example, counted 34,500 chemical accidents in the United States between 1988 and 1992. During the same time period, chemical accidents at plants and during transportation claimed more than five hundred lives and caused almost three thousand injuries. As Bhopal showed, these statistics are minor compared to what can happen in other parts of the world.

Today, the U.S. Chemical Incident Reports Center online database lists almost daily chemical spills and fires. These range from the most dramatic "boiling liquid expanding vapor explosions" (BLEVEs), as when a railway chemical tanker blows up, to the many on-site spills that are relatively small in scope. According to the Emergency Planning for Chemical Spills website:

> One in twenty of the chemical accidents that occurred in the United States resulted in immediate injuries, evacuations, or deaths. Anhydrous ammonia, chlorine, sulfuric acid, sulfur dioxide, and hydrochloric acid were the chemicals most frequently involved in accidents with immediate injury, evacuation, and death.[6]

▼ Train derailments leading to chemical spills from tank cars, such as happened in Milligan, Florida, in 1979, often result in injuries and require evacuations.

One reason for the frequent incidents relates to the size of the industry, especially in the United States. The numbers are staggering, with fifteen thousand facilities producing, storing, or using potentially dangerous amounts of 140 of the deadliest toxic chemicals.

Another reason for the persistence of chemical accidents relates to a disturbing tendency for incidents to recur at the same repeat-offender facilities. According to a recent study of oil and chemical facilities in California's Contra Costa County:

> Many of the serious incidents and major accidents at Contra Costa County refineries are due to recurring problems at certain process units that remain unresolved and result in continuing accidents. An examination of County records for 1999 and 2000 shows that, over and over again, incidents occurred in the same problem areas, even after the facility claimed to have solved the problem and resumed operations.[7]

One company that suffered an especially embarrassing repeat incident was Union Carbide. Less than a year after Bhopal, a chemical release eerily similar in its cause—errors in the handling of chemicals being stored in large tanks—occurred at Union Carbide's plant in Institute, West Virginia. Some four thousand pounds of the chemical aldicarb oxime escaped into the air and drifted over a residential area, sending more than one hundred people to the hospital for eye and lung irritations. This same Bhopal sister plant has experienced subsequent accidents as well, including a 1999 spill, resulting from a gasket failure, of 133 pounds of the lung-irritating gas phosgene. Compared to the twelve-thousand-pound spill of a similar gas in Bhopal, it was a small spill. Twenty years ago, it probably would not have been reported. Now the law requires it.

THE PUBLIC'S RIGHT TO KNOW

In 1986 Congress enacted the Emergency Planning and Community Right-to-Know Act (EPCRA). Administered by the EPA, the law is designed to help citizens and communities know exactly what chemicals are stored or manufactured in nearby facilities. Hospitals and paramedics can therefore have antidotes on hand for emergencies, and devise treatment and rescue plans. Citizens can look at evacuation plans, safety and inspection reports, and spill reports. If an accident occurs, the facility must notify various authorities and provide, among other information, the name of the chemical, an estimate of the quantity released into the environment, and any known or anticipated acute or chronic health effects. If industries do not comply, the law helps citizens sue either the industry or the government agencies.

Pipes Not Safe Enough

The worst chemical spills have occurred at production facilities, but others also regularly occur during transport of chemicals. Of the twenty-eight serious U.S. pipeline ruptures the NTSB has investigated since 1990, most have involved dangerous chemicals or petroleum products. These pipes can be huge and cause havoc. In 1997 a Louisiana jury found plastic pipe manufacturer Condea Vista guilty of spilling, over eight months, 19 to 47 million pounds of ethylene dichloride from its own pipes into local waterways around Lake Charles. Ethylene dichloride is a toxic chemical used to produce polyvinyl chloride (PVC) plastic pipes. Exposure to ethylene dichloride can cause nausea, vomiting, and irritation to the skin or eyes; over time it may lead to cancer or damage the liver, kidneys, or nerves.

According to a report from Greenpeace, "The Chicot aquifer, which supplies drinking water to southwest Louisiana and southeast Texas, now contains seventy-six times the safe limit of ethylene dichloride."[8] Greenpeace has petitioned the EPA to block applications for other plastic pipe facilities being sought in the Lake Charles area.

▲ Residents of the Lake Charles, Louisiana, area contend that chemical spills from vinyl manufacturers, such as the Condea Vista facility shown here, have contaminated the local water.

Long-Term Time Bombs

Chemicals, much like crude oil, may be so toxic in high concentrations during the initial stages of a spill that they can cause acute and immediately deadly effects. As chemicals, oil, and other toxic substances age, break down, and are dissipated or diluted by water and wind, most of their toxic effects diminish. Certain of their compounds, however, can cause long-term health problems as they move through the food chain to accumulate in animals and people. The concentration of toxins, from tiny organisms to larger animals and even to humans, can allow thousands or even millions of times the original dosage of poison to be consumed by predators ranging from alligators to great blue herons at the top of the food chain. This is called bio-accumulation, a twist of nature that reverses dispersal. Instead toxins are reconcentrated and repackaged in the food supply.

The most feared disease of long-term toxic exposure is cancer, and it is also the most complex and controversial. When a carcinogenic chemical enters the body, it has the potential to cause cell mutations and to damage DNA, which affects how cells reproduce. Scientists are unsure, however, exactly how much of any toxic substance is required, and for how long of an exposure, for cells to begin to mutate. Moreover, animals, people, and different populations of people respond differently to carcinogens. Often many years pass

▶ Great blue herons prey on everything from small fish to snakes, putting them near the top of the wetlands food chain and thus especially vulnerable to the buildup of oil and chemical toxins.

HOW TOXINS BUILD UP IN THE FOOD CHAIN

The three scientist-authors of *Our Stolen Future* offer a stark description of how bio-accumulation of the hazardous chemical PCB occurred in Lake Ontario. The chain began with simple microorganisms. Their consumption of PCB molecules increased the density of the toxin by 500-fold. Tiny shrimp that ate the microorganisms increased the original PCB density by a factor of twenty-five thousand. Smelt, which are small fish, ate the shrimp and increased the density by 855,000-fold.

Along came lake trout that gobbled the smelt, multiplying the PCB density by 2.8 million. Gulls who also ate the smelt increased the original PCB concentration by 25 million, illustrating how different organisms store poisons differently. The PCBs did not kill the large predators, however. Instead, the chemical acted like a deranged hormone, disrupting the development of the predators' eggs and causing deformed offspring and much lower birth rates.

before cancers become active, thus making tracing of the original cause difficult.

Birth defects and nervous system diseases may also take years after the initial exposure to cause damage. Birth defects result from DNA errors, cell mutations, or disrupted hormonal messages that strike fetuses as they are first developing. Nerve or brain damage is of special concern because nerve cells do not repair themselves or regenerate, even though the toxins that caused the damage may be flushed from the system.

The path of a toxic spill is thus filled with twists and turns, surges and ebbs. After the initial shock and acute damage, the spill may seem to go into hiding. But it still moves, regroups from its dormant slumbers, and creeps into the tiniest particles of life, affecting the DNA code that dictates the behavior of dividing molecules. Here the toxins, diluted beyond detection, do their most insidious work: turning the body into its own enemy.

Old Messes, Lengthy Consequences

One grim example of long-term effects occurred at the site of Claremont Polychemical on Long Island, New York. The company went broke in 1980, leaving three thousand leaking drums and storage tanks. With a long unrecorded history of spills, Claremont produced and used a toxic cocktail of

▲ The Italian tanker *Ievoli Sun* spilled nearly 2 million gallons of toxic chemicals before sinking during an Atlantic storm in October 2000.

solvents, pigments, vinyl stabilizers, and metal flakes such as asbestos. One of their most lethal chemicals, tetra-chloroethene, a solvent often used in the dry cleaning indus-try, had leached into the ground and contaminated drinking water in the area. The EPA identified the abandoned mess as a Superfund site and proposed a series of remedies in a 1990 report.

The EPA estimated that without taking action, the site would pose a risk to human health for a hundred years. At a cost of about $6 million to remove contaminated soil, the EPA estimated that the threat to health could be reduced to sixty-two years. A more expensive alternative, involving excavating soil as well as digging wells to suck the poisons from the groundwater plume, would cost nearly $29 million. The EPA estimated that, even pursuing the more expensive option, it could take sixteen years of work and monitoring before drink-ing water in the aquifer would likely be safe.

There are thousands of such sites, long since abandoned by bankrupt companies, with no spill records, no reliable lists of toxic substances, and no clear production histories essen-tial for assessing damage and devising cleanup strategies. Many of these operations spilled for years, leaving long-term plumes of poison widely dispersed and thus often much more difficult to fix than more dramatic, headline-grabbing sudden disasters.

Chemicals Harder to Predict

Compared to land spills, chemicals spilled in water pose even more complex and varied problems. This is because some chemicals are diluted by water, some react with water, some escape into the air, some are carried by water to new destinations, and some are simply not predictable. For example, in October 2000, an Italian tanker sank off the coast of Cherbourg, France, spilling nearly 2 million gallons of toxic chemicals, including 1.3 million gallons of styrene (a chemical used to make plastics) and several toxic solvents. The owners of the aging ship did not know what to do, so the British government sent a navy minesweeper to locate the vessel. Officials also began to work on a plan to salvage the chemical cargo and to prevent or reduce any environmental damage.

When the minesweeper arrived, finding the sunken ship in 214 feet of water turned out to be easy. The crew could smell the styrene above the wreck. Unlike oil, however, they could not see floating styrene or estimate how much had leaked from the hull. They had no comparable experience and were literally working in the dark.

It turns out that smell is a useful indicator for identifying properties of spilled toxic chemicals. Scientists in New Mexico have invented an "electronic nose" that uses sensors to sniff out clusters of odors and to infer the characteristics of the spill. The sensors identify not only the types of chemicals and how they may mix but also the changing concentrations during dispersal.

From this data scientists can create a map showing dispersal plumes and thus figure where chemicals are moving, how they are being diluted, and how their toxic properties are changing. Orchestrating a cleanup can begin only when the nature and behavior of the spill are clear, a first step that is often more difficult with chemicals than it is with oil.

Peril Along the Rails

Train wrecks account for some of the most memorable chemical disasters. A single railway tanker can carry twenty thousand gallons of chemical products. Derailments, accidents at

REVENGE OF THE EARTH

Chemicals can sometimes act in unpredictable ways to come back and haunt their makers. Florida is a major producer of phosphate, which is used in fertilizers. Industrial phosphate production generates vast amounts of toxic contaminants, which phosphate companies often store in huge, highly acidic wastewater lakes. In 1994 one such chemical lake in Florida, after 20 million pounds of liquid phosphoric acid had been dumped into it over many years, began eating the very earth below it. Suddenly, almost as if the earth itself were sending an angry message, a giant hole more than a hundred feet wide and nearly two hundred feet deep opened, allowing the contents of the chemical lake to sink in a bizarre whirlpool "like a scene out of Jules Verne's *Journey to the Center of the Earth*," said the Fluoride Action Network.

This example of chemical leaching on a most dramatic scale was a very dangerous spill, threatening the local water table and contaminating two major wells owned and used by the plant. The company was forced to seal the great hole with concrete and then plug it a year later at a cost of $6.8 million.

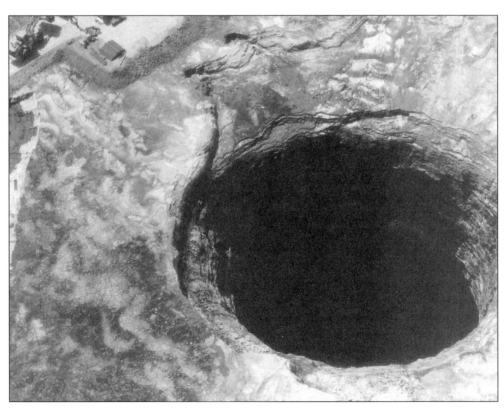

▲ This gaping hole is the result of millions of pounds of chemicals being dumped into a wastewater lake.

traffic crossings, collisions, and tanker car malfunctions can lead to spills or explosions. "Many rail yards also were laid out along rivers and lakes," noted the *Wall Street Journal*, "making the consequences of spills that much worse."[9]

▲ A number of chemical fires erupted when a freight train derailed and exploded in February 1996 about sixty miles east of Los Angeles.

One of the most environmentally damaging chemical spills in U.S. history happened on the night of July 14, 1991, when seven cars derailed as a train was negotiating a sharp curve near Mount Shasta in northern California. One of the cars that jumped the tracks was a tanker. It plunged off a bridge and into the Sacramento River below, where it broke open and spilled its entire contents of nineteen thousand gallons of the herbicide metam sodium. The chemical readily mixed with the water and began to flow toward Lake Shasta, forty miles away.

Soon the river downstream of the spill stank of dead trout and other fish. Songbirds, otters, mollusks, insects, and other wildlife died. Soil along the river was poisoned, the aquifer was contaminated, and plants died. A scientific report noted that "virtually every aquatic organism on a 40-mile stretch of river was killed, setting the biological stopwatch back to zero."[10]

In the aftermath of the spill authorities evacuated the nearby town of Dunsmuir, plus some residences along the Sacramento River. They also closed a stretch of interstate highway that paralleled the river. More than forty cleanup workers who had helped to remove dead fish from the river reported skin irritations, but otherwise there were no injuries to humans.

A Robust Response

Five years later, the Sacramento River ecosystem was still affected, but this once-thriving trout habitat was well on the way to recovery. The U.S. Fish and Wildlife Service, along with state and private partners, negotiated a settlement with the parties responsible for the spill. A portion of the $38-million assessment was earmarked to restore damaged natural resources, monitor spill recovery, and acquire nearby habitats to replace those lost during the spill. Ideally such spills can be prevented, but in this case an effective government response, deep community concern, and strong scientific follow-up were evidence of a robust sociocultural correction in the system.

Of the approximately forty serious railroad accidents investigated by the NTSB since 1996, a quarter have involved spills of hazardous chemicals or waste that have lead to injuries, deaths, and area evacuations. Most of the accidents resulted from mechanical breakdowns or procedural and human errors. The NTSB reports invariably call for changes and improvements in rail systems, training, and inspections, suggesting that nearly all such accidents are preventable. It is impossible to know how many accidents are prevented as a result of these grim experiences. But learning one accident at a time is a slow process.

The Spills of War

Facing defeat in the 1991 Persian Gulf War, Iraqi dictator Saddam Hussein ordered his retreating troops to intentionally spill oil from terminals and tankers of the Saudi Arabian and Kuwaiti coasts. The result, 460 million gallons of oil spilled, was the worst oil spill in history. Iraqi troops also set fire to almost seven hundred oil wells. In the 2003 Iraq War, Iraqis again set fire to a number of oil wells. Today, various Arab governments are concerned that their facilities could become terrorist targets. So despite international agreements prohibiting environmental damage during armed conflict, deliberate oil spills and fires have become weapons imposing vast environmental damage and economic trauma.

One consequence of the 1991 oil spills and fires was an increase in the price of oil, which eventually led to a worldwide recession. Continuing political turmoil in the Middle East throughout the 1990s also led to a terrorist attack that changed the world. Jetliners that crashed into the two World Trade Center towers on September 11, 2001, served as explosives whose heat and impact caused the collapse of these massive buildings. The toxic cloud that resulted added to this horrible human tragedy.

The explosive potential of some chemicals, in combination with their deadly fumes, pose an even greater terrorist threat. On the eve of the 2003 Iraq War, Homeland Security secretary Tom Ridge told CNN that terrorists could use chemical plants as a weapon. "There is no question that when we take a look at a chemical facility, the possibility that terrorists could use that economic asset and turn it into a weapon is something that we need to be concerned about and are concerned about,"[11] Ridge said.

In 2003 Congress's General Accounting Office released a report warning that 700 chemical facilities could potentially

▲ Oil well fires in northern Kuwait burn out of control behind a destroyed Iraqi tank after the 1991 Persian Gulf War.

threaten at least 100,000 people, and each of about 3,000 facilities could potentially threaten at least 10,000 people. As a result, security at chemical plants has become an important new component in the spill prevention arsenal. Conceivably, the 12,000-gallon Bhopal spill could pale in magnitude to a truck bomb set off in any major chemical facility located near urban centers.

Quenching the Treacherous Spill

When the Iraqi army ignited 656 Kuwaiti oil wells in 1991, no one had ever seen anything comparable. The sun vanished behind thick, roiling black clouds. Blue sky was replaced by an eerie, oily night. Upwards of 73 billion gallons of oil "flared off into the sky or dumped in thick, tar-like lakes at the rate of six million barrels a day. . . . Snow in the Himalayas would be blackened by the falling particles carried by high altitude winds. Sheep, a thousand miles away, would have their coats covered in a sticky brown residue,"[12] according to the *Petroleum Economist.* As the oil and soot spread over surrounding desert, the sand and gravel congealed into vast patches of hardened "tarcrete" that covered almost 5 percent of Kuwait's area.

These fires and the few that were set in Iraq during the second Gulf War were easy to start with explosives rigged to the wellheads. The explosions ignited the oil, which spewed into the air under enormous pressure. The volatile spray burned like a powerful blowtorch, immune to conventional firefighting methods or equipment.

The effects were long-term and wide ranging. The wells burned for nine months and emitted five thousand tons of soot, 1 to 2 million tons of carbon dioxide, nine thousand tons of sulfur dioxide, and an undetermined amount of toxic chemicals. Breathing of the fumes by soldiers downwind is suspected to have contributed to Gulf War Illness and was recently recognized by the U.S. Department of Defense as a factor in the illnesses and disabilities reported by a hundred thousand Gulf War veterans. It is now believed that the oil field fires, in combination with exposure to nerve gas released during demolition of an Iraqi munitions depot, are responsible for chronic health problems.

Red Adair to the Rescue

Oil well firefighter Red Adair has been honing his craft since the 1940s, helping to put out major fires such as the *Ixtoc I* oil

◀ Texan Red Adair, shown here on his way to fighting a blowout in Norway in April 1977, is one of the world's foremost oil well firefighters.

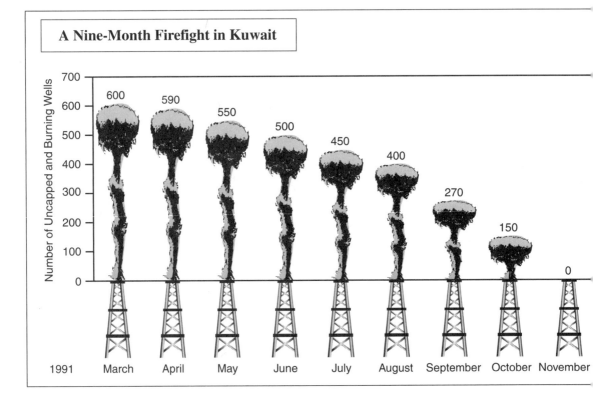

A Nine-Month Firefight in Kuwait

Number of Uncapped and Burning Wells

1991	March	April	May	June	July	August	September	October	November
	600	590	550	500	450	400	270	150	0

rig blowout in 1979. He became a legend in his home state of Texas, where his crews doused blowout fires by the dozens. Even so, he had never faced anything like the numerous well-head fires still burning in the Kuwaiti oil fields during the weeks following the January–February 1991 Persian Gulf War. Toxic fumes sprayed into the sky in volumes never before imagined. In an arid locale with minimal equipment, withering heat, and lethal land mines sprinkled everywhere, Adair began a task that experts feared could take many years.

For nine months Adair and his crews extinguished blazes and capped wells. Finally, in early November 1991, the worst oil disaster in history was brought to a halt. Although Adair garnered international acclaim and widespread publicity, teams from six other countries joined the effort. Perhaps most notable was the Wild Well Killers, a team organized by thirty-two-year-old Kuwaiti oil engineer Sara Akbar. Of what would eventually be ten thousand firefighters, Akbar was the only woman. Later featured in the IMAX film *Fires of Kuwait*, she became a heroine in a country not noted for liberated women.

Kuwait's Oil Heroine

Prior to the Kuwaiti oil blazes, Sara Akbar refused to flee from the Iraqi army. She stayed at her post as an oil engineer through the invasion, even though she had just married and was risking her life. Iraqi soldiers plundered offices and records. Eventually Iraqi explosives experts sought plans for the 940 Kuwaiti oil wells. The Iraqis escorted Akbar to the well sites, and she quickly realized that the information they sought was for the purpose of blowing up the wells. So when she returned home from her excursions, she notified the Kuwaiti underground about the wells being wired. These resistance fighters went from well to well, disconnecting the charges.

More of the wells could have been saved if an exiled Kuwaiti oil minister had not boasted to the Arab press about the brave efforts of the resistance fighters. Just prior to the beginning of the international coalition's offensive to free Kuwait, the Iraqis read the accounts and rushed back into the Kuwaiti oil fields to rewire the wellhead explosives. Fortunately, they did not have a chance to rewire at least one hundred wells, reducing the scope of the ultimate disaster. Once the coalition troops drove away the Iraqi army, Akbar recruited a team of Kuwaiti firefighters to help put out the blazes.

The overall price tag for the Kuwaiti oil fires was $1.5 billion to fight the fires, and $10 billion of lost oil revenue. Much of the environmental wreckage remains evident today. Thus, when American and British troops returned to Iraq in 2003 to remove Saddam Hussein from power, this time they were ready to avert environmental disaster. Troops rushed to protect Iraqi well fields, preventing all but nine oil wells from going up in flames. Nonetheless, Iraqis set fire to oil-filled ditches and human-made

HOW TO FIGHT A WELLHEAD FIRE

Squelching an oil well fire is somewhat like trying to put out a building-sized blowtorch. In Kuwait, firefighting teams managed to extinguish some of the first fires by making use of a converted oil pipeline. Instead of transporting oil to the Persian Gulf, engineers reversed the flow direction and sent massive volumes of sea water to the burning oil fields. There the firefighters rigged jet airplane engines to battle tanks, and sprayed fires with water from the powerful jet turbines. Another method was to raise the level of the wellhead flame, by installing massive pipe casings over the wellhead so that the oil had to travel up through forty feet of pipe before igniting. With the flame extended into the sky, frigid liquid nitrogen and water were pumped downward into the well, cutting off oxygen.

▶ In March 2003, twelve years after the end of the Persian Gulf War, a Kuwaiti government official collects a sample from a crude oil lake formed during the conflict.

ponds around the capital city of Baghdad, hoping that the billowing clouds of noxious smoke would hinder American bombing. So once again spills became weapons of war. But this time, soldiers knew more about prevention, and the horrid effects if they failed.

Tiny Particles, Big Consequences

The effects on human health from the 1991 oil field fires remain speculative. Researchers are still studying the disaster, with the 2003 Iraq war adding to the growing knowledge base of chemical and oil spills. According to the *Boston Globe*, "Health specialists say the biggest concerns in the [oil cloud] mixture are tiny particles that are small enough to lodge in lungs and cause respiratory damage"[13] that can have long-term consequences.

Today, scientists remain uncertain as to whether oil fires alone caused Gulf War Illness. Other contributing factors may have included demolition of a chemical weapons storage depot and the mix of inoculations soldiers were given to protect them against disease and biological weapons. Multiple factors could be at work, as could tendencies some soldiers may have had for lung or nervous system disorders that were then triggered by toxic exposure.

Could these conditions be caused by other factors not related to the war? The Department of Defense takes the following position:

> This is a very difficult question to answer because cancer and other common ailments, which account for 70 percent of all illness reported by Persian Gulf veterans, may occur with increased frequency in individuals following exposure to a variety of toxic substances. Cancer, however, may require twenty to thirty years to develop following a toxic exposure.[14]

In the 2003 Iraq war, the UN attempted to monitor the smoke and pollutants given off by the few oil well fires and by the burning lakes and trenches of oil in and around Baghdad. The U.S. military also gathered much baseline medical information before sending troops into combat. This data may help sort through the environmental consequences of war and help clarify the effects of oil toxins on human health.

The Mystery of Chemical Demolition

In March 1991, the Gulf War recently over, soldiers blew up a large ammunition depot at Khamisiyah in southern Iraq. Defense officials later learned that the nerve agents sarin and cyclosarin had been stored in the depot, and were almost certainly released into the air. U.S. government officials tracked almost all of the one hundred thousand Gulf War veterans who had been in the region at the time of the demolition and warned them they might have been exposed to low levels of these chemical agents.

▲ The September 11, 2001, terrorist attack on New York City has had long-term environmental effects.

In recent years the U.S. government has slowly acknowledged that Gulf War Illness, characterized by skin conditions, lung damage, chronic fatigue, and stress disorders, does exist. The two primary causes are thought to be the nerve gas agents from Khamisiyah and the particles from the nine-month-long oil fires. But exactly how these agents affect people over many years is difficult to pin down. In perhaps another consequence of war, researchers are able to study the combined effects of oil and chemical disasters that will yield answers that apply to civilian accidents.

Eyewitness to Chaos

It was 8:50 A.M. on September 11, 2001. New York City writer Lee Gruzen was in her bedroom tidying up, ready to go out into a glorious sunny day, the door to her apartment less than a two-minute walk from the two World Trade Center (WTC) towers. Suddenly, the room shook with tremors that felt like a dreadful earthquake. Gruzen rushed down to the street, where neighbors had already gathered. They all stared up hundreds of feet into the sky where flames poured from the upper stories of one of the WTC towers. "We were trying to figure out what was happening, and we could see these tiny people, like tiny stick figures, flopping almost gracefully in the bright blue sky. They were so tiny," she said. "We realized they were falling."[15] Thus began an unimaginable nightmare.

Soon afterward, Gruzen and her neighbors saw a huge jet-liner "curve over our heads, and with a little flourish of its wings, straightened and smashed into the second tower. It was a huge explosion. That's a sound I'll never forget," she said. "It was just awful."[16]

Gruzen went into a ground-floor supermarket to buy emergency supplies and reached the soup section when people rushed in the door screaming, "The building's coming down! The building's coming down!" Then a huge cloud rushed past the windows, at first a "glorious sun-lit whiteness, then a blizzard, then darkness swept by, a huge wind roaring past that seemed to suck the life force out of the city,"[17] delivering in its wake a gruesome aura of death that would last for weeks.

Finally there came "a snowstorm of gritty, dead white debris like cornmeal,"[18] Gruzen recalls. It piled ankle deep as the acrid air, smelling of chemicals and fried electrical circuits, stung people's throats. Gruzen and her husband, who had been working nearby, made their way to the waterfront, where dozens of boats nosed up to the bulkhead to aid in the evacuation. They stepped into a dive boat that had been repairing the piers, hundreds of people pouring onto a makeshift fleet, leaving scores of empty baby carriages abandoned on the wharf.

Chemical Effects of 9/11

Four days later, the world stunned, the rubble of two massive towers still burning, police escorted the Gruzens back to their apartment. The cleanup was massive, with giant cranes and powerful machines digging day and night, a great din of "muscular power of men and machines" and the gradual return of a "profound life force,"[19] said Lee Gruzen. It soon became clear to her and others, however, that the collapse and burning of the two World Trade Center towers, in addition to being a sudden catastrophe, was also a long-term oil and chemical disaster.

After being struck by the terrorist-guided jetliners, the two skyscrapers pancaked into 3 billion pounds of smoking debris. Flames from super-heated jet fuel engulfed the upper stories, spewing toxic hydrocarbons and chemical additives. Thousands of gallons of burning oil from the towers' heating systems emitted a nonstop cloud of petrochemicals. Dust from concrete, asbestos, and crushed debris sprinkled down on the city like volcanic ash. Tens of thousands of gallons of transformer oil laden with PCBs burned. Satellite images revealed the toxic cloud extended over Brooklyn all the way to Coney Island.

Less than a month after the disaster, EPA officials were reassuring the people of Manhattan that the city's air was safe to breathe. This was in spite of the fact that fires continued to smolder beneath the mountain of rubble, and the increasing numbers of New Yorkers who were complaining of throat and lung irritations. It was not until February 2002 that researchers from the University of California-Davis confirmed the extent of the pollution. In October 2001, they had measured for very fine particles of uncommon air pollutants, such as nickel, vanadium, and titanium. These toxic metals, which may have originated in vaporized computers, airplane parts, and so forth, are so rarely airborne that EPA tests had overlooked them. The tiny size of the particles made them even more hazardous to health, since they could easily lodge in the lungs. Combined with the dangerous levels of airborne sulfuric acid, lead, asbestos, silicon, and other pollutants, the WTC disaster ranked as the single worst air pollution episode in U.S. history, the UC-Davis researchers concluded.

By the spring of 2002, New York's air was back to pre–September 11 status. By then, however, over 90 percent of firefighters involved in the cleanup were complaining of respiratory and related illnesses. A year later 350 firefighters remained on medical leave. One estimate is that ten thousand New Yorkers suffered health effects related to the post-disaster pollution. The initial response to September 11 concentrated on the horrific death and destruction, but the environmental trauma may haunt for many years.

World Trade Center Cough

Medical researchers warned that perhaps the greatest long-term danger of the WTC's toxic spill would be fine dust particles that seeped into nearby buildings to embed in rugs, drapes, cracks, and crevices, and that could be stirred into indoor air for years. A year after the disaster a new disease, "World Trade Center Cough," emerged. Dr. Walfred Leon of SUNY Downstate Medical Center said, "We've never encountered anything like this before in medicine."[20] He said the chemical complexity of the debris and smoke exceeded anything heart and lung specialists had previously seen. While the EPA found only a few examples of high levels of asbestos and PCBs in the air of nearby buildings (the poisons they most feared), other researchers found asbestos embedded in nearby office furniture, drapes, and rugs, a potential long-term threat to health.

The World Trade Center disaster illustrates the difficulty of dealing with mixed toxins during an unprecedented catastrophe. The EPA in particular did not see the cleanup of apartment buildings and workplaces as being central to their role. New York congressman Jerrold Nadler ripped the EPA at a public hearing, saying a year and a half after the attack: "The EPA is condemning some people to die fifteen or twenty years from now from lung cancer and mesothelioma [a type of tumor]. The EPA must stop stonewalling, and finally carry out its legal and moral responsibility to clean up all buildings contaminated in the terrorist attack."[21]

Acts of war, terrorism, and disaster place scientists and the government under special pressure. Soldiers, firefighters, and rescue workers enter disaster scenes willingly, and they expect support for their heroic efforts. When doubts arise about later illnesses, their rage carries a special moral force. Yet, in the chaos and immediate trauma of such events, attending to long-term issues is only an emerging consideration that researchers now see requires rapid response.

When Terrorists Strike

The events of September 11, 2001, focused the world's attention on the potentially devastating effects of terrorist attacks not only on skyscrapers but also on ships transporting oil or chemicals. This fear proved well-founded. In October 2002 the

▲ The waterline hole in the hull of the *Limburg* is visible in the background as a U.S. anti-terrorism expert photographs journalists off the coast of Yemen in October 2002.

French oil tanker *Limburg* was rammed off the coast of Yemen by a boat packed with explosives, spilling and burning 3.7 million gallons of oil. Despite warnings by maritime officials that civilian vessels could make easy targets for the notorious terrorist Osama bin Laden, the *Limburg* had no security escort when it was attacked. French investigators found traces of TNT. Bin Laden wrote, "By striking the oil tanker in Yemen with explosives, the attackers struck at the umbilical cord of the Christians, reminding the enemy of the bloody price they have to pay for continuing their aggression against our nation."[22]

In the wake of the *Limburg* terror attack, U.S. intelligence officials called for increased security on oil tankers and in ports to prevent similar marine oil spills. The U.S. Coast Guard has recently begun providing armed escort services to tankers carrying oil, gas, and other potentially dangerous cargoes as the ships enter and leave U.S. ports. These are costly efforts, however. Given the great number of ships transporting oil and other toxic materials, protecting them from terror attacks poses huge challenges. In Boston Harbor, for example, the Coast Guard now escorts liquefied-gas tankers to massive storage tank farms at the edges of the city. The fear is that a small powerboat laden with explosives could detonate a ship and the tank farm, leveling portions of downtown Boston.

Pipelines in Harm's Way

Oil tankers are not alone in their vulnerability to terrorist attack. Oil pipelines move much of the world's oil, and many are in politically volatile locations around the world. U.S. Special Forces stationed in Arauca, Colombia, were sent there in part to protect Colombia's main national pipeline, hundreds of miles long laced through steamy jungles. The pipeline has been attacked more than a thousand times by anti-government guerrillas. Meanwhile, construction of the Baku-Tbilisi-Ceyhan (BTC) pipeline in the Caucasus region of Georgia and Azerbaijan near Russia may be halted due to fears of sabotage resulting from ethnic rivalries in the region.

A nearby Azerbaijan pipeline linking Baku oil fields to the Black Sea was damaged by sabotage, spilling up to 160 tons of oil and raising concerns about the BTC project. Pipeline ruptures as acts of war or terror do not gather much publicity, but they represent a major problem. More dangerous chemical and natural gas pipelines represent additional targets for terror and war, and, due to their length, are more difficult to protect than industrial plants.

Chemical Disasters Waiting to Happen

Chemical plants pose many of the same challenges as oil tankers and pipelines when it comes to protecting them from terrorist attack. Consider the Kuehne Chemical Company plant in South Kearny, New Jersey, which is only nine miles from New York City and prides itself as the world's largest producer of chlorine-containing hypochlorite bleach. The plant produces 200 million gallons of hypochlorite bleach a year and is capable of storing a million gallons. It is a major producer of sulfur dioxide, which reacts explosively with chlorine if accidentally mixed. It also stores, sells, and transports hydrogen, a

▲ Oil pipelines in central Asia, like this one at the Black Sea port of Supsa, Georgia, are vulnerable to sabotage.

powerful explosive. The worst-case accident scenario that the company submitted to the EPA showed that the facility puts a larger population (12 million people) at risk from an accident than any other chemical plant in the United States. The company stresses that safe operations is a high priority, but government officials have expressed alarm that Kuehne and plants like it are not more secure from terrorist assault.

In January 2003, reporter Jake Tapper visited the Kuehne plant to check out its security against terrorism. Tapper was shocked to discover that the plant had "relatively flimsy-looking" electronic gates and chain-link fences, manned by security guards that "aren't that daunting."[23]

The Kuehne plant has begun to address the need for greater fence-line security, but Congress recently rejected efforts to mandate increased security at chemical plants. Intense industry lobbying helped to defeat the legislation, critics charge. The congressional General Accounting Office warned in March 2003 that the U.S. government, including the EPA, "has not comprehensively assessed the chemical industry's vulnerabilities to terrorist attacks."[24] The GAO report praised the industry for initiating some voluntary efforts, and urged the EPA to use the civilian requirements of the Clean Air Act to tighten chemical plant security.

In today's strife-torn world, oil and chemical facilities represent major targets in armed conflict. As symbolic centers of power and wealth, they are also prime targets for destruction by terrorists. They provide the inexpensive raw materials of terrible bombs and have thus become favored by the weak in their assault on the mighty. Only recently has the U.S. government recognized that such facilities contain the home-grown bomb materials that would be nearly impossible to smuggle across the borders. "I just believe that at the end of the day, it's a lot easier getting something that's already here in the United States than trying to sneak in sarin,"[25] the assistant secretary of Health and Human Services warned Congress in April 2003. Environmentalists contend that, ultimately, oil and chemical companies need to take the further step of using safer materials, thus neutralizing altogether their desirability as terrorist targets.

▼ A security guard stands by a chlorine tank in a chemical plant near Belgrade, Yugoslavia, in April 1999, after plant officials warned that any bombing of the facility could cause an environmental disaster.

CHAPTER FOUR

Response and Cleanup

As long as there are chemical plants and oil facilities, there will be spills. The best prevention plans, technology, training, expertise, science, regulations, laws, and human concern can, at best, minimize spills. But once they do happen, the best hope at preventing outright disaster is rapid, intelligent response and prompt, professional cleanup. Some of this is done in advance with emergency response and cleanup plans required by national and local agencies. Systematic tracking of cleanup events builds experience and knowledge. Training and money are crucial. Supervision and leadership play a huge role, and science points the way for reducing harm.

In the United States, those responsible for oil and chemical spills must report incidents immediately to the Coast Guard's National Response Center, which mobilizes a half dozen federal agencies for immediate reaction. The EPA plays the leading role in responding to spills. It can quickly organize technical experts, including biologists, chemists, geologists, and engineers, to provide around-the-clock assistance at the scene of an oil or chemical spill.

Many first responders are local emergency workers who may, or may not, be trained for these disasters. HAZMAT (hazardous materials) teams that include local as well as federal responders are organized, trained, and funded in some states but not all. Nonetheless, federal law requires industries to develop emergency spill plans, and together these efforts can increase the speed, professionalism, and thoroughness of initial response and cleanup.

Oil and chemical spill responses differ in several key respects, the most important being the prompt and expert medical attention essential to chemical accidents. Many chemical spills also often require evacuation of people and pose dangerous conditions for rescuers and cleanup crews that can delay or hamper cleanup. But in many respects, the principles are similar for oil and chemical spills, and the first order of business is to stop the spill and prevent its spread.

Top Priority: Containing the Source

Once an oil spill occurs, companies and government agencies first must contain the spill by trying to block the source and stem the flow of any unspilled fuel. Officials may face difficult technical decisions when a wrecked or disabled ship still contains large quantities of oil. Among the most commonly used options is lightering—off-loading the oil into another ship. Factors such as the weather, ocean conditions, and how the ship has ruptured can make lightering difficult or impractical.

For spills into water, various options may be used. In situ burning (setting the oil on fire) can reduce the oil's adverse impact on water but releases pollutants into the air. More commonly, containment booms are moved into place around the oil slick. These are floating barriers, comparable to giant

▼ The EPA set up a log boom to hold back oil polluted water on the San Juan River in 1972.

▶ Off-loading of oil or fuel, such as the burning freighter *Pallas* was able to do to a platform in the German North Sea in November 1998, can sometimes prevent a major spill.

inner tubes, that extend about three feet below the water surface and prevent the oil from dispersing. Then skimmers, much akin to vacuum cleaners, are moved in to suck the oil off the water for safe removal. But the best solution is to stop the spill quickly.

If the spill reaches shore, cleanup crews must work quickly, since oil that seeps into soils is beyond the reach of surface absorbents and most other products. At the same time, medical teams must protect workers exposed to fumes and oil-drenched skin as they work under difficult conditions.

Various onshore technologies can be mobilized, including high-pressure steam cleaners, chemical detergents, and biological agents that "eat" the oil, causing it to break down into less harmful by-products. Companies such as Dawg of Middlebury, Connecticut, specialize in selling high-tech absorbents akin to fancy sponges in a vast array of configurations, such as socks, pillows, pads, and rolls, that both contain and soak up oil. Even such low-tech devices as mops are deployed to soak up small pools of oil.

But none of these processes is perfect. For example, steam and detergents can thin the oil, driving it deeper into soils or into the body of water, where toxins are released and continue to kill organisms. Biological agents are limited in how much oil they can consume, and bad weather often disperses oil beyond the booms and out of reach of skimmers.

Rescuing Injured Animals

The rescue and cleaning of oil-saturated birds and sea mammals is also an imperfect process. Oil has a devastating effect

▼ Fishermen use low-tech scoops to skim up oil spilled from the *Prestige*.

on animals and needs to be quickly removed to save their lives. For example, oil clinging to birds prevents them from preening and aligning their feathers. When birds' feathers are not precisely overlapping, birds lose their natural abilities to fly, stay warm or cool, and remain buoyant in water. Even a small, dime-sized patch of oil on a bird is enough to kill it.

One remarkable rescue effort that illustrates the danger of oil on feathers occurred after a 2000 oil spill off the coast of Tasmania, south of Australia. Hundreds of "little blue" penguins, the smallest penguins in the world, were doused in oil and began dying. Rescuers started knitting tiny sweaters and issued a worldwide call for help. Soon fifteen thousand sweaters arrived, and rescuers dressed the twelve-inch-tall birds. According to the Tasmanian Conservation Trust, "Oil clogs the feathers of these tiny seagoing birds, and reduces their insulating and waterproofing qualities. Even worse, the penguins attempt to clean themselves by preening, and rapidly become poisoned."[26] The knitting project worked, and the leftover outfits have been stored in oil spill rescue kits. Oil-soaked flying birds, however, need to be washed.

In order for containment, cleanup, and animal rescue technologies to work well, response must be rapid, expertly coordinated, and aided by luck. Fortunately, most countries have a range of environmental groups, scientific organizations, and private enterprises that can provide the know-how, experience, and people power to carry out much of the cleanup. Government agencies typically play a crucial role in supervising and coordinating everything from the placement of containment booms to the rehabilitation of injured birds. The result when done well is significant mitigation of the disaster.

OIL SPILL BIRDBATHS

Cleaning oily birds is an arduous and delicate task. Already stressed and dehydrated, these birds are often near death, from freezing, malnutrition, or ingestion of the toxic oil during preening when rescued. According to the International Bird Rescue Research Center in Fairfield, California, the birds must first be given nutrients and gentle care. "Once stable, oiled birds go through a series of tub washes alternating between baths with a one percent solution of Dawn dishwashing liquid and clean water. The wash time varies depending on the amount of oil, and the size of the bird, but on average it takes two people forty-five minutes and three hundred gallons of water to do a thorough washing." The birds are then warmed, dried, and monitored until they are healthy and have restored their own natural waterproofing.

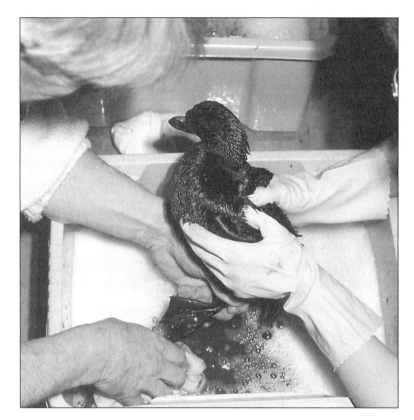

◄ Bird rescuers clean oil from the feathers of a black scoter duck caught in the February 1996 *Sea Empress* spill off the coast of England.

When a Pipeline Bursts

A different set of challenges is present when oil is spilled on land, such as from a pipeline rupture. Simply detecting pipeline ruptures can be tricky. Unlike a tanker accident, where the spill is usually quickly obvious, pipeline spills can flow into the ground in remote areas where there are few people to notice. For example, in April 2000, more than 140,000 gallons of oil leaked from a supply pipe at the Chalk Point Generating Station, Maryland's largest power plant, before it was discovered. By then oil had dispersed into nearby wetlands, creeks, and the Patuxent River, causing a mess that cost $71 million to clean up. An NTSB investigation of the Chalk Point spill found that the company's flow monitoring system was not sensitive enough to pick up a 140,000-gallon shortage of oil flowing into the power plant, and that the company's spill response system was not adequate even when the spill was discovered.

An even more remote pipeline spill occurred in October 2001, when a drunken man armed with a high-powered rifle shot a hole in the Trans-Alaska Pipeline about seventy miles north of Fairbanks. A surveillance helicopter spotted the spill within hours but more than 285,000 gallons of crude oil sprayed out of the pipeline at high pressure over the next twenty-four hours before the leak was finally stopped. The pipeline needed to be shut down for three days so that emergency crews could patch it. The spill was the among the worst in the pipeline's history and the first to be caused by a bullet.

Cleanup crews spent months removing soil and replanting trees over three acres of oil-contaminated land next to the site of the spill. In this case, a number of factors worked to limit the environmental damage and promote effective cleanup. For example, few animals were affected. Also, because the ground was almost frozen, much of the oil stayed pooled on the surface, allowing for the use of absorbents. Even so hundreds of workers were involved in the cleanup and it cost more than $3 million.

Storage Tank Spills

Oil storage tanks pose another set of cleanup difficulties. For example, on January 13, 2003, the National Response Center received a report that up to twelve hundred gallons of hydraulic oil had spilled from the Profile Fibers plant in Hickory,

MAKING DIRT CLEAN

In 1989 an abandoned transformer plant in Fayetteville, North Carolina, was discovered to be leaking PCBs, dioxins, and other contaminants into the soil. The EPA declared the area a Superfund site and excavated 975 tons of contaminated soil that was leaching into the drinking water wells of three thousand nearby residents. Rainwater runoff was also contaminating a watershed draining into the Cape Fear River three miles away.

After the initial cleanup, the EPA contracted with San Diego–based Terra-Kleen to clean the soil at the site. Terra-Kleen uses mobile, on-site technology to remove oil or chemicals from soil before rainwater can sink down and disperse the toxins, thus preventing them from doing any further damage. The company loaded soil into large bins and treated it with nontoxic solvents that dissolved some of the contaminants. Filters captured other toxins, ultimately leaving clean soil that could be used as backfill. The EPA installed pumps to extract contaminated groundwater nearby, and hooked residents to a clean water system. Using multiple technologies, an extremely dangerous spill was finally stopped, and the area restored.

North Carolina. The spill occurred as a result of a fire at the facility two days earlier. It had damaged two hydraulic oil storage tanks, allowing oil to be released into two small catch ponds at Profile Fibers. The ponds then spilled over into a small creek.

Cleanup workers contained the spill and checked for seepage into the ground, a major concern in land spills. In very large spills, the underground dispersal plume must be tracked. When possible, wells are drilled to extract oil and clean groundwater soils, especially if drinking water is involved. Eventually, the oil in soil often finds its way to water, as rain seeps downward and begins to disperse it.

The underground water spreads and flows like ink spilled on blotter paper. At the same time, water flows downhill, along rock strata in ways comparable to surface water in streams and lakes. An underground aquifer is made up of water pooled in the midst of sand and soil, like a saturated sponge. Drinking wells tap into these sources of water. If oil has dispersed into the spongy mass, it contaminates the drinking water supply. To avert further contamination of the creek in the Profile Fibers case, the EPA required that the company hire a cleanup contractor, one of thousands around the country specializing in toxic and oil cleanups.

The ultimate goal of pipeline and storage tank spill cleanups is to bring ruined land, often referred to as brownfields, back into productive use. A number of states have sought help from the EPA in repairing brownfields at shutdown military bases drenched with spilled munitions, fuels, and toxins. In 2001, for example, the Fort Wayne, Indiana, Air National Guard completed all required environmental cleanups at its facilities. But rather than let these former toxic wastelands remain idle, Indiana began to re-develop these brownfields. The state "provides community assistance in several different forms," the state's lead environmental agency reports. "To date, approximately 105 Indiana communities have received brownfields funding and/or other assistance for approximately 245 sites to be redeveloped and returned to productive economic reuse."[27]

Chemical Cleanup Challenges

The greatest challenge with chemicals is the much greater likelihood, compared to oil spills, of quickly lethal effects at the spill site, resulting from explosions or high concentrations

▲ Volunteer firefighters don protective suits before entering the damaged West Pharmaceutical Services plant, with its many hazardous materials.

of toxins. Once a chemical spill occurs, the spilled agent needs to be identified and the dangers calculated. The spill must be safely stopped, and people responding must don protective gear, including masks and special suits. Rescue teams must be called in to help treat and remove those injured.

Emergency response workers may test the concentration of a chemical so that cleanup specialists can calculate evacuation and treatment options. If exposure to a highly toxic substance is possible, people need to be warned and populated areas evacuated. Also, the environmental consequences must be tracked, first as an acute threat to people's lives, and then for the potential long-term damage to health and community safety resulting from chronic exposures.

An example of this frantic jumble of challenges was a fire and explosion at a West Pharmaceutical Services plant in North Carolina in January 2003. The blast shook the whole city of Kinston, sending flames hundreds of feet into the air. "Some residents of Kinston, N.C. thought a plane had crashed into the local airport, while others were certain they were experiencing a major earthquake. What they felt yesterday afternoon was actually a devastating explosion at a medical supply company,"[28] wrote Sandy Smith for the Occupational Hazards website. It took all day and night to put out the fire, delaying cleanup or hazards investigations. Four people died and thirty-seven were injured from the explosion and fire.

The plant manufactured syringes and intravenous devices, seemingly innocent enough products, but they used some nasty chemicals in the process. After the fire was put out, the EPA discovered 107 hazardous materials at the site, including methylene chloride, chloroform, hydrogen sulfide, and a variety of solvents, although none in massive quantities. Previous inspection of the site indicated an inadequate emergency plan and resulted in warnings that chemicals used there posed a threat to human life in the event of an accident.

Federal investigators later speculated that the cause of the fire may have been a cloud of pulverized rubber particles that accidentally ignited. At the time of the explosion, the scene was chaotic. The first priority was rescuing workers and putting out the fire. When the emergency phase ended, the EPA monitored air and water quality, removed chemicals, cleaned up numerous site spills, installed dams in drainage basins, and monitored the chemical runoff that ended up at the city sewage treatment plant. Unlike an oil spill, even a relatively small chemical accident confronts everyone with a myriad of scary unknowns.

Disaster in France

Large chemical disasters sometimes involve frightening dangers, such as the explosion of a fertilizer factory in Toulouse, France, on September 21, 2001. Registering 3.4 on the Richter scale, comparable to a small earthquake, the blast killed 30 people, injured 2,400, and caused the evacuation of 15,500 residents including children from 90 schools. The disaster was France's worst industrial accident in 50 years. It impacted 300,000 more people, with effects ranging from a massive toxic cloud to contaminated drinking water. Subsequent investigations have suggested that the cause was probably a mistake in the mixing of chemicals.

Even a month after the blast, "Thousands of homes surrounding the plant are still without roofs, windows and even walls. Temporary caravan parks have sprung up on the outskirts of the city,"[29] according to a BBC report. The cleanup operation led to more local outrage when thousands of dead fish were discovered in the river that flows past the industrial site, apparently killed by liquefied ammonia the plant was dumping into the river. The devastation from the explosion was so vast that Toulouse authorities prevented a neighboring plant from continuing to operate one of its more hazardous units.

▼ Two firefighters help an injured worker from the wreckage of the French fertilizer plant that suffered a massive explosion in September 2001.

Diverse Strategies Needed

Response agencies must also quickly diagnose how the chemical spill is being dispersed. Because chemicals are so diverse in makeup, no single technology, such as the containment booms frequently used in oil spills, can be counted on. Chemicals may be solid, liquid, or gas, and when exposed to air or each other, may dissipate or react violently. Often spills result from or cause fires, unleashing poisonous clouds moved by the wind. Spills into streams or water pose other dispersal problems, moving poisons quickly yet also diluting and changing toxic properties and victims' symptoms as they spread. Chemical companies must therefore have plans, antidotes, equipment, and emergency strategies in place in anticipation of spills' unique effects.

The Occupational Health and Safety Centre in Mumbai, India, publishes a manual of antidotes and treatments for chemical exposure that illustrates the complexities. It includes antidotes for scores of common chemicals, each with varying effects depending upon how long after exposure the antidote is given. It then offers detailed first-aid instructions for how to restore breathing, stem bleeding (including internal), test for nerve damage, evaluate and treat burns, and deal with trauma injuries. For each chemical hazard, different treatments are required, different steps and precautions are prescribed.

A chemical plant using various toxins must have plans and procedures for every possibility. The manual warns, "It is to be noted that usually the victim comes with exposure to a mixture of chemicals, hence if prior knowledge is lacking regarding the chemicals he is exposed to, it is impossible to diagnose a specific chemical toxicity in the emergency setting."[30] In short, if plans and treatments are not readily available before the fact, the victim is in trouble.

When Threats Multiply

Even with extensive emergency plans prepared in advance, chemical spills are unpredictable and each one presents unique challenges. Many accidents may involve threats from multiple agents. That was the case not long after midnight on November 19, 1991, when twenty-eight railcars in a freight train derailed on a bridge near the small town of Shepherdsville, Kentucky. Three of the derailed railcars contained

▲ The extent of the damage from the Toulouse explosion has raised questions about the siting of chemical plants.

hazardous cargo: the chemical MDI used in manufacturing plastic, the insect killer POX, and U.S. Army cluster bombs.

When the EPA coordinator arrived, she faced a critical situation. The POX car might explode at any moment and the vapors from the leaking MDI were a threat, at high temperatures, to release an extremely toxic gas. Residents, workers, and students within a one-mile radius were evacuated, fully half the town. The responders decided quickly that the major concerns were putting out the fire and preventing an explosion.

Quick attention to these multiple threats, plus a bit of luck, led the EPA to close the case with little environmental damage reported. For a relatively small spill such as Shepherdsville, skilled rapid response can work. For a massive explosion such as in Toulouse, the destruction is simply overwhelming, and many cities in France are considering no longer allowing large facilities near populated areas.

Protection against civilian accidents must begin by finding out what facilities are close enough to pose a threat, and what chemicals are used or stored. Terror threats with chemical weapons are not predictable, however, so having a radio and cell phone ready for emergencies is crucial.

The Challenge of Urban Cleanups

Oil and chemical spills that occur in metropolitan areas, where toxins can take multiple paths that might cause human exposure, can present additional cleanup challenges. In June 1994, arsenic acid leaked from a rusty railway tank car at a Norfolk Southern Railway yard in Chattanooga, Tennessee. Workers grabbed what they could—in this case, a children's swimming pool—to contain the poison, but three thousand gallons of the acid escaped. Some even got into the yard's drainage system and eventually into the Tennessee River, near intake pipes for the city's municipal water supply. A major public health disaster was averted but the incident highlighted the dangers of poor emergency planning, as well as faulty inspection by the wood preservative manufacturer that leased the tank car.

Urban chemical spills that occur at night pose special risks, since detection may be slowed and sleeping residents are less able to respond rapidly to toxic clouds. It is especially important, therefore, that industries and response agencies have a clear map of the potential spill footprints or plumes. Computer models are used to predict how spills behave with different chemicals under different circumstances. One of the most popular computer programs, developed by emergency respond ers at NOAA and now distributed worldwide to thousands of users in government and industry, is Areal Locations of Hazardous Atmospheres (ALOHA). It is widely used for response, planning, training, and academic purposes.

"ALOHA can predict rates of chemical release from broken gas pipes, leaking tanks, and evaporating puddles, and can model the dispersion of both neutrally-buoyant and heavier-than-air gases,"[31] according to NOAA. For example, ALOHA can show

WHAT TO DO DURING A CHEMICAL EMERGENCY

Government agencies have developed guidelines for how to prepare for various types of toxic spills. The Federal Emergency Management Agency (FEMA) advises citizens to identify two meeting places, one near home and the second away from the neighborhood in case home cannot be approached. Find out the emergency response plans of employers, school, day care, and other officials, and where they would evacuate workers and students. Have a plan for pets, since shelters do not allow them. Assemble a "disaster supply kit," including bottled water, food, and emergency supplies. Keep a first-aid kit at home and in vehicles. If necessary, turn off air conditioning and retreat to a safe, secure room with duct tape, emergency radio, and plastic sheeting. When the crisis is over, FEMA says that citizens should follow decontamination instructions from local authorities.

that ammonia creates twice as large a spill footprint as benzene for the same size spill over the same duration. The size of the spill also affects the size of the footprint in predictable ways. Thus, five hundred pounds of ammonia travels five hundred yards whereas fifty thousand pounds travels one and a half miles. At night in cool temperatures, the same ammonia plumes travel more quickly and with less dissipation by sunlight and air temperature. Hence, at night, ammonia spills are more dangerous. With very little wind, the plume is broader, but add a twenty-mile-per-hour wind, and it turns from a fat blob into a narrow dart. In the city, the plume travels 25 percent more slowly than in open country. These variables can affect the safety and evacuation of thousands of people in an urban setting.

These models can forecast evacuation strategies, medical response, containment, and cleanup far more quickly than on-the-ground monitoring. "ALOHA also allows the user to make concentration and dose location calculations. This function allows the responder to determine what the level of a spilled chemical will likely be at a particular location downwind from the spill,"[32] reports Chemicalspill.org. The program can even predict how quickly gaseous plumes will seep into buildings. Calculations done in advance of spills, based on various scenarios, thus save lives and allow rapid, targeted cleanup far from the original spill site. By knowing the weather and the chemicals, responders can know how to react to a spill without even seeing it.

Lingering Effects

After the initial, messy, and concentrated spill, nature helps to clean up. Oil and chemical fires spill into the atmosphere and poisons are carried hundreds of miles by wind. Ocean and coastal spills are battered by waves and wind, then spread by currents. Pipeline ruptures and land-based spills are absorbed by soil and seep into the groundwater. In some cases this natural dispersion dilutes toxins and reduces the local threat to health. In other cases it can spread poisons into foods or water that people eventually consume, potentially getting concentrated in living tissue.

A similar pattern emerged with the *Exxon Valdez, Amoco Cadiz,* the *Argo Merchant,* and many other massive spills. Nature proved handy at cosmetic cleaning, but oil is a poison

TRACKING THE TOXINS

In order to be effective, cleanup workers need to know what happens to toxins as they disperse into soil and water. To evaluate the complex routes that toxic substances take through the environment, scientist R.L. Metcalf simulated a pond using a ten-gallon aquarium containing sandy soils, plankton, algae, snails, mosquito larvae, plants, and fish.

Suspected toxins were spilled into the tank, and after about a month, several dozen larvae, then water fleas, and mosquito fish were introduced in three-day intervals. Soon everything was removed and tested. The outcome allowed scientists to predict the flow of toxins through the ecosystem and to take steps during cleanup to intercept the toxins before they entered the food chain. Metcalf's pioneering models launched the new science of ecotoxicology and offered important insights into how toxic substances move over time through the food chain.

that contaminates bacteria, plankton, algae, and tiny critters in the intertidal zones crucial to the breeding of fish, shrimp, crabs, and the small-fry members of the greater food chain. Despite the massive initial kills, specie recovery in Alaska after the *Exxon Valdez* spill has been remarkable. Lingering effects, however, still persist, with genetic defects showing up in ducks and other species.

Today toxicologists play an important role in risk management, a process for weighing the risks of toxic substances against their benefits. Risk management attempts to measure costs, determine safety standards, and develop regulations for use, storage, transport, manufacture, and cleanup. "Relatively few environmental toxicants have no useful function," says toxicologist B. Magnus Francis. "Therefore, every decision to ban a chemical carries a cost or a risk of its own."[33]

Gender-Bending Toxins

Scientists have also discovered important new knowledge during and after the cleanup process. For example, in 1980 a waste pool spilled over from a pesticide factory near the shore of Florida's Lake Apopka. Large amounts of DDT and dicofol contaminated the lake. Soon after the spill, 90 percent of the lake's alligators died. Fifteen years after the cleanup, the alligators had returned very slowly. On average, only one out of five of their eggs hatched, versus nine out of ten for normal alligators.

Scientists puzzled by the low birth rate took to the water at night in air boats and captured alligators for testing. University of Florida biologist Louis J. Guillette Jr. determined that most of the male alligators had abnormally small reproductive organs. Blood tests revealed that the male animals had significantly reduced levels of the hormone testosterone, similar to the low levels normally found in females. This confirmed scientists' suspicion that the pesticides could mimic the effects of the female hormone estrogen.

The class of toxins called hormone disrupters can confuse the body, inducing changes in cell development at key times, leading to breeding problems and birth defects. While the alligators were otherwise healthy, their hampered capacity to breed threatened their survival. The alligator findings caused such concern that the EPA called a meeting of toxicologists and biologists around the world to discuss and develop new research strategies for looking at the lingering hormonal effects of toxic chemicals passed up through the food chain.

Scientific analyses can play an important role in reducing the risk of spills and charting the effects of toxins at every stage of their impact on health and the environment. While modern society's current reliance upon oil will not last forever—as a natural resource, it is being used up faster than nature can replace it—chemicals are simply too useful to replace. They will not only be here for the duration of advanced technological society, but they will evolve and multiply, exposing the earth to new dangers and new advances. Understanding these substances thoroughly is a key to cleanup and recovery.

CHAPTER FIVE

Preventing Oil and Chemical Accidents

A number of important safety reforms have been prompted by disasters such as the *Exxon Valdez* spill and the Bhopal leak. Some of these are technical fixes, such as building more durable ships, better plants, and safer railroad cars. But replacing old technologies takes time and money, and unsafe clunkers still ply water and rail. Regulations have also sought to address issues relating to work rules and employee training. Fines and penalties have been increased for unsafe practices, giving teeth to regulations and laws. The environment has become its own industry, with companies offering solutions for anyone willing to invest.

Programs in the United States such as the federal Oil Spill Liability Trust Fund go beyond cracking the whip, offering help to industries and increasing their stake in spill prevention. In 1985 the EPA created its Chemical Emergency Preparedness program to encourage state and local authorities to identify hazards in their areas and to plan for potential chemical emergencies. Congress also soon enacted rules relating to emergency response plans that, for example, require facilities to make information available to the public on the hazardous chemicals they have on-site.

Environmental groups hammer away at lax industries but also increasingly offer praise for safety innovations and risk reduction. Citizens groups and government officials have begun to closely coordinate their efforts, and new technologies are being marshaled to reduce the risk and damage of spills.

Still, years of neglect and the steady growth of the oil and chemical industries make prevention all the more urgent.

Diverse Forces at Work

One of the challenges of spill prevention is the complexity of regulatory processes for protecting people and the environment against careless handling of oil and chemicals. The U.S. government has dozens of agencies involved in the licensing, supervision, enforcement, research, and oversight of oil and chemical manufacturing and transportation. Many other governments around the world have comparable agencies. States have their own more localized versions of regulatory agencies, and industry associations and organizations also define standards and performance. The massive regulatory effort is necessary because oil and chemical spills present so many long-term challenges.

Moreover, dozens of nonprofit advocacy groups, such as the Sierra Club, Greenpeace, and the Environmental Defense Fund, watch for spills, new pollutants, and dangerous conditions. They regularly sue companies and government agencies, and inform the public about their findings. Nonprofits often call upon the thousands of scientists from universities around the world who study spills and track environmental and health effects.

Engineering firms that specialize in spill prevention often send teams to oil and chemical facilities to recommend risk reduction strategies. For example, Dvirka and Bartilucci Consulting Engineers in Woodbury, New York, offers an Accidental Release Prevention Program. Its engineers look at a plant's spill history and analyze manufacturing, storage, hazard risk, and community response plans to help oil and chemical companies redesign their facilities to stop accidents before they happen.

Enviro Shield Products in Yuma, Arizona, builds custom devices to capture, contain, or prevent spills. It visits facilities at risk for spills and designs preventive devices to fit a manufacturer's needs. Another company, Ship and Shore Environmental of Signal Hill, California, manufactures "thermal oxidizers" that convert toxic chemicals and gases to carbon dioxide and water, thus eliminating waste storage, transport, and disposal. These types of products and services allow many facilities to modernize and eventually save money through spill prevention.

Prevention Through Innovation

One of the best strategies to avert or reduce disaster is prevention through innovation. The Chemical Manufacturers Association (CMA) argues that the industry is making progress in reducing spills and chemical releases. One success the association cites is the effort at Union Carbide to dramatically reduce acetone leaks in pipes at a plant in Texas City, through a combination of repairs and improved worker training. ICI Americas of Wilmington, Delaware, provides another example. Instead of continuing to use potentially toxic cadmium and chromium in pigments for plastic resins, it developed a new pigment free of heavy metals. The CMA says that a number of companies have developed new ways to recycle toxic wastes, reducing or eliminating dangerous waste storage, disposal, and shipping steps where many accidents occur.

Environmental groups, which can be sharply critical of the chemical industry, also praise industry innovations.

▼ Engineering firms offer site assessment services that may involve identifying and disposing of toxic chemicals.

According to the Washington, D.C.–based U.S. Public Interest Research Group (U.S. PIRG), "Choosing inherently safer technologies—modifying production or products to use safer or fewer chemicals, reduced chemical quantities, or processes involving safer pressures, temperatures or other conditions—reduces or eliminates the possibility of a chemical release."[34] A prominent example cited by U.S. PIRG is Dupont's decision, after the 1984 Bhopal accident, to eliminate storing methyl isocyanate. Instead its plants began to use a closed-loop process that only produces as much of the deadly chemical as is needed at the time.

Double the Protection

One potentially useful preventive measure that governments agree on relates to the benefits of double-hull tankers. These have a number of advantages in preventing oil spills compared to single-hull ships. Both the United States and the European Union (EU) have adopted regulations requiring newly built oil tankers to have double hulls. Shortly after the disastrous *Prestige* oil tanker spill off the Spanish Coast, French president Jacques Chirac lamented to French reporters, "I am horrified by the inability of those in charge, politically, nationally, and particularly at European level, to take action to stem the laxity which permits ships fit only for the dustbin to carry on."[35] European Union transport ministers responded by approving an immediate ban on single-hull tankers that try to carry heavy fuels, like crude oil, into EU ports. A total U.S. ban will not go into effect until 2015, although bills have been filed to speed that up. Meanwhile, some two thousand aging single-hull tankers, more than half the world's tanker fleet, continue to transport 30 billion gallons of oil a year around the world.

The early evidence suggests that double hulls are effective —most of the oil spills in the past decade have involved single-hull tankers. The eventual switch to double hulls will not, however, be a panacea. Salt water that gets into the space between the two hulls can corrode structural frameworks. The World Wildlife Fund warns:

> It is also worth remembering that double-hulls have their own inherent problems. Many predict that in a few years time we will be seeing massive oil spills from double-hull tankers as the maintenance of a double-hull is more difficult than a single-hull, and there is also a problem with gas build up between the two hulls.[36]

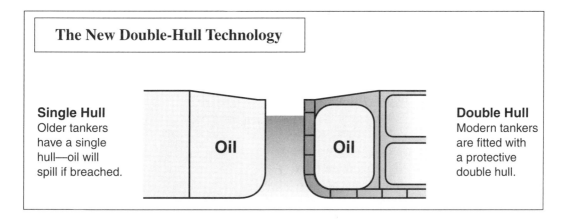

The New Double-Hull Technology

Single Hull
Older tankers have a single hull—oil will spill if breached.

Oil

Oil

Double Hull
Modern tankers are fitted with a protective double hull.

This concern is reflected by the London-based Oil Companies International Marine Forum, which states, "Double hulled tankers may only be the answer if combined with high quality operation; maintenance; classification surveys; and proper policing by flag state and port state."[37]

Clearly the days are numbered for oil tanker rust buckets. But even double hulls cannot prevent spills when ships run hard aground on rocky shoals. Nonetheless, newer ships will also be equipped with state-of-the-art navigation systems, and the number of horrendous spills should continue to decline.

Wielding the Threat of Punishment

Legal steps to help prevent spills include more potent fines and penalties. Steep penalties prompt companies to pay more attention to environmental concerns. Lawsuits were quickly filed against Exxon after the *Exxon Valdez* disaster in 1989. On September 16, 1994, a federal jury ordered Exxon to pay $5 billion in punitive damages, the largest punishment ever against a corporation, for its role in the disaster. The jury also ordered the former ship captain Joseph Hazelwood to pay five thousand dollars in punitive damages. It is worth noting that these judgments were awarded in spite of the fact that Exxon helped to clean up and study the spill.

In another example, a Norwegian shipping company pleaded guilty in 2003 for negligence in a twenty-three-thousand-gallon oil spill off the South Carolina coast in 1999. The shipping company admitted that its ship discharged a "harmful quantity" of oil into the ocean, according to the U.S. attorney's office in Columbia, South Carolina. The oil killed 183 birds, mostly loons, which washed up on the

ASSIGNING BLAME AT THE TOP

Although the Bhopal disaster was defined as an industrial accident, the safety violations, faulty manufacturing processes, and degrees of negligence were so pronounced that the Indian government filed a number of lawsuits against Union Carbide (now owned by Dow Chemical). Indian officials also arrested then Union Carbide chief executive officer Warren Anderson, who had come to Bhopal after the accident. Released on bail, he left the country and has never returned. A Bhopal court has nevertheless had several summons served on Anderson, now retired and living in Bridgehampton, New York, for "culpable homicide"—being responsible for causing the death of another person or persons—and other crimes. In 1992 the court began to press the Indian government to request that the U.S. government forcibly deliver the "fugitive from justice" to India for trial. So far, the Indian government has stalled requesting that U.S. officials extradite Anderson. Nevertheless, it is clear that, almost two decades after the accident, many of the people of Bhopal remain angry at both Anderson and Union Carbide.

▲ A blind victim of the 1984 Bhopal tragedy holds an accusatory placard during a December 2001 commemorative rally.

beaches of North and South Carolina. The company paid a half million dollars, most earmarked for conservation efforts in the area affected.

Some lawsuits attempt to prevent disasters before they happen. The National Environmental Law Center (NELC), a nonprofit project that was started to take enforcement action against the nation's worst polluters, found out that Dow Chemical was storing thousands of tons of cancer-causing dioxins in waste pools at a facility near Michigan's Saginaw Bay. To prevent a spill, leak, or accident that could have catastrophic consequences, the center successfully sued under the Clean Water Act to force removal of the dioxins and cleanup of the site. When the company delayed, the NELC sued again and, in July 2001, forced a $1 million fine and creation of a $30 million waste disposal program requiring all dioxins to be removed to a licensed landfill. "Dow must meet a series of loading, handling, transport, disposal, and monitoring requirements specified by the citizen groups,"[38] the lawyers wrote.

The NELC has racked up a series of similar court victories in recent years, including a $2 million penalty against the P.H. Glatfelter paper company of York, Pennsylvania, for industrial discharges in a local creek. The money was used to fund a watershed endowment project. In the mid-1990s the center also won a consent decree (a judgment requiring compliance with the law) against the Department of Defense preventing it from spilling oil, grease, raw sewage, and toxic chemicals into Washington's Puget Sound. Although lawsuits are expensive and time consuming, they remind industries that spills can be bad for business. Lawsuits are also a tool of last resort to force enforcement of existing laws. Public service law firms, such as NELC, provide citizens extra leverage against companies tempted to cut corners.

Funding Oil Spill Prevention

Largely in response to public outrage over the *Exxon Valdez* incident, the federal government passed a comprehensive new law targeted at improving the nation's ability to prevent and respond to oil spills. The Oil Pollution Act of 1990 expanded the federal government's ability to respond to oil spills. The law also consolidated funding for the four-year-old Oil Spill Liability Trust Fund. The OSLTF collects money from a five-cents-a-barrel oil tax and from interest on fund principal. The trust fund also assesses monetary penalties on parties responsible for oil spills. As a result, up to $1 billion per spill incident is available from the OSLTF to respond to crises, pay claims, and restore damaged resources.

In 1999 and 2000, the fund opened more than 1,300 cases and billed oil spillers for $40 million in damages and costs. By the end of 2000, it had filed 38 lawsuits and secured nearly 14,000 pledges of responsibility from shipping companies, which said that they would be accountable for the costs and cleanup of spills. By the end of 2000, the fund had handled 6,100 oil spill cases seeking $420 million in damage payments.

NEVADA'S HAZARDOUS MATERIAL SPILL CENTER

The federal government's Nevada Test Site, some seventy miles northwest of Las Vegas, has not been used to test nuclear bombs for more than a decade, but it is now the site of a one-of-a-kind facility for testing hazardous materials and training response crews. From April through September, weather permitting, the Hazardous Material Spill Center uses live releases of toxic chemicals to field-test detection equipment, protective gear, and procedures. The center's facilities include a ninety-six-foot-long wind tunnel to study plume releases, a tank farm for simulating liquid spills, and outdoor "spill pads" where chemicals can be released under realistic scenarios. There are also indoor "test cell areas" where materials and instruments can be exposed to high concentrations of test materials. Private companies can rent the facility to test products and technologies.

A key aspect of the program is to put potential oil polluters on notice that they must pay for their spills, thus driving up the costs and accountability for accidents, a crucial incentive for prevention. Moreover, it also enforces existing laws and can ban vessels from ports, nullify their shipping licenses, and can exact penalties of up to $27,500 per day for noncompliance. In addition, the fund provides information and workshops to help shippers comply with laws and safe practices.

What is unique about the fund is that it enlists cooperation from industries in advance of trouble and helps them to comply with standards. It offers a carrot and a stick and thus dramatizes that compliance pays dividends. Many laws and regulations are mostly stick, resulting in industries resenting government intervention.

Railways Respond

The shipping industry is not alone in its attention to technical fixes: Railroads stung by heavy fines and cleanup costs are now using safer cars with armor plate, and refueling stations are being built with "double-bottom tanks, double-wall pipes, spill pads and alarms that warn of spills."[39] Following the 1991 Sacramento River chemical spill, concrete barriers were erected along rails to protect sensitive areas near streams and lakes. Better procedures, computerized navigation and rail systems, and better training can also help to prevent rail disasters.

Rail yards "are among the most contaminated sites in the country," says John DeVillars, former New England regional administrator of the EPA. "They've just never gotten the same attention that other big dirties got."[40] Some two thousand rail yards in the United States, many in environmentally sensitive or urban areas, handle both petroleum products and toxic chemicals. Many industries also have their own loading and off-loading facilities. As with ships, rail transfers of fuels and chemicals pose opportunities for error or equipment failure. Rail yards are busy places, often built on stone and gravel bedding where spills quickly disappear undetected into underlying soil. Railway tankers carrying fuels and chemicals move frequently, so a leaking railcar may be difficult to trace. The pattern of environmental neglect at most rail yards, however, is slowly changing.

While prevention is now getting new attention, the railway industry faces the challenge of dealing with untold numbers of dormant spill sites. One such site was recently discovered in Elkhart, Indiana, through the determination of a diverse group of neighborhood activists. Citizens League for Environmental

▼ Emergency responders practice fire fighting at Nevada's Hazardous Material Spill Center.

▲ Railway leaks due to accidents or natural disasters, like this tanker damaged by a California earthquake in January 1994, represent serious environmental threats.

Action Now (CLEAN) prompted the EPA to investigate the water quality in their area, not far from Conrail Railyard. The group suspected that wells were contaminated from a largely forgotten sixteen-thousand-gallon spill of carbon tetrachloride that the rail yard had experienced two decades earlier. When water tests confirmed dangerous levels of chemical contamination, the area was declared a Superfund site, and residents were hooked to safe public water supplies. Prevention can help reduce or end a legacy of neglect, but dormant spills of this kind are hidden beneath rail beds in perhaps hundreds of locations that threaten the health of nearby residents.

High-Tech Eye in the Sky

The European Space Agency's March 2002 launch of Envisat, the world's largest and most sophisticated earth observation satellite, has given scientists and government officials a powerful new technology for tracking oil spills and prosecuting polluters. As Envisat circles the earth in a five-hundred-mile-high orbit, its state-of-the-art radar imaging technology can take detailed, wide-swath pictures showing, for example, ocean circulation, ice cap activity, and environmental pollution. Satellite images of oil spills can lead to spill response in less than two hours, the European Commission reports, and "are useful not only for eventual prosecution of pollution culprit, but also for more strategic monitoring for developing oil spill indicators and thus establishing trends in marine oil pollution."[41] Tough enforcement and new knowledge about trends are crucial for devising prevention strategies.

Envisat images were used to track the November 2002 *Prestige* spill off Spain, and showed the plume approaching the Spanish coast. It alerted authorities to the movement and behavior of the spill, and while winds proved an insurmountable obstacle in preventing massive shoreline damage, the images allowed authorities to respond quickly. An added advantage of the satellite radar is the ability to see through rain and fog, common elements in weather-related spills that often cannot be tracked by conventional aircraft. "This unique capability allowed Envisat's ASAR [Advanced Synthetic Aperture Radar] to 'see' the oil leaking from the

A CONGRESSMAN WHO MADE A DIFFERENCE

On May 31, 2002, two hundred gallons of deadly hydrochloric acid leaked into the Concord River from a railroad tanker car near Lowell, Massachusetts. The relatively small spill prompted Massachusetts congressman Marty Meehan to declare, "Federal regulations are where we are going to fix this." The Federal Railroad Administration, which regulates hazardous chemicals transported by rail throughout the country, and the tank car owner investigated the reason for the leak. Their analysis identified extensive failures in the rubber lining designed to hold the chemical inside the tank car. When the lining leaked, the acid ate a hole in the metal of the tank car, and escaped onto the ground. A similar pattern of lining leaks, due to the lining not being cured at the time of application, was identified in other cars. In this case a single congressman's response to "the tragedy that almost happened in Lowell," along with the actions of a federal agency, helped to shape railway policy and prevent a much larger accident.

tanker despite heavy rain and cloud cover in the region that hindered the coverage of optical instruments,"[42] reported *SpaceHike.com.*

The European Space Agency has said that it will make Envisat images available as part of the International Charter on Space and Major Disasters. The charter is an agreement to offer the use of satellite technology whenever civil protection agencies think it can be useful in the aftermath of a natural or man-made disaster.

A World of Risk

Clearly a common concern running from spills, to response, to cleanup, to prevention is the need to understand more about chemical behavior when something goes awry. Industrial chemists have been brilliant in understanding and producing chemical products that work, but when the process fails during dramatic spills and their aftereffects, chemicals leap out of the lab and into the dark side of nature.

Such is the imperfect science and regulatory control of oil and chemical products, and their many ways of spilling into the food chain and ultimately reaching humans. It is a world of risk, of progress, of mistakes, of enormous regulation, of advanced science and medicine, of thousands of laws, and of armies of lawyers battling for public and private interests. But massive spills will not end.

The good news is that science and painful experience are making inroads on all aspects of spills. Governments have responded with increasing sophistication to these threats, and, compared to thirty years ago, are light-years ahead of where they were. Technology—the practical, nuts and bolts application of science—has emerged with a vast array of gadgets and engineering solutions for prevention, cleanup, and restoration. And industries are increasingly seeing that prevention can pay off in profits.

The bad news is that accidents still happen, many industries remain unwilling or unable to stem the tide, and governments often lack the will or political support to push harder for expensive remedies. The developing world, especially, remains vulnerable to the expensive preventive and cleanup measures required for protecting themselves. With more and more companies moving into developing countries where labor is cheap and regulation more lax, keeping a lid on disasters may prove far more difficult.

The highly developed industrial world, meanwhile, faces new threats of terrorism and the difficult reality that facilities were often located years ago in the wrong places, undermining public safety. Despite improved technology, many ships, rail cars, pipelines, and manufacturing facilities are simply old and obsolete. And too often environmentalists, governments, and industries fight each other rather than work toward common goals.

▼ This photo taken by the Envisat satellite tracks the pathway of spilled oil as it snakes from the *Prestige* tanker to the Spanish coast.

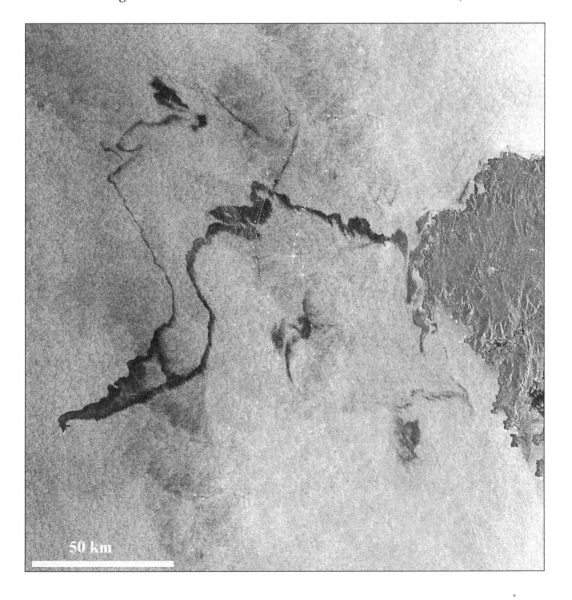

50 km

▲ A stream boom at a Rhode Island spill restoration project helps to monitor progress and test nature's resilience.

Testing Nature's Resilience

Ultimately, the oil component should largely go the way of the dinosaur to be replaced by cleaner, safer energy alternatives. But chemicals are here to stay, and the lawyers on all sides are sharpening their swords. In the balance are great new products, life-saving medicines, the abundance of the world's food supply, the birth of healthy babies, clean and abundant drinking water, fresh air to breathe—the fate of the planet and its ecosystems. Spills will continue to happen, some catastrophic, but increasingly, ignorance is no longer an excuse.

The systems and science for vast improvement are well established. How people respond will decide the lives and health of thousands and perhaps millions of people for years to come. It would be no small irony if all these substances, extracted from the earth's basic building blocks, turn around and destroy the planet or many of its major life forms. It would seem that spills alone could not do this, but spills are only part of a much bigger landscape. They are the insults and injuries, the body blows to an environment whose overall fitness and resilience will decide the future of the planet.

Notes

Introduction: Large-Scale Disasters

1. Quoted in Jake Tapper, "America's Achilles' Heel," *Salon.com*, March 18, 2003. www.salon.com.

Chapter 1: Oil Spills

2. Richard Charter, "The Renewable Roadmap to Energy Independence: Prepared Statement, Field Hearing of the Subcommittee on Energy," February 21, 2002, *The Democratic Caucus Committee on Science*. www.house.gov.
3. Yereth Rosen, "Exxon Valdez Oil Still Harmful, U.S. Studies Say," *Environmental News Network,* January 15, 2003. www.enn.com.
4. *U.S. Environmental Protection Agency*, Oil Program, "Ashland Oil Spill." www.epa.gov.

Chapter 2: Deadly Chemicals on the Loose

5. Dominique Lapierre and Javier Moro, *Five Past Midnight in Bhopal.* New York: Warner Books, 2002, p. 378.
6. *Emergency Planning for Chemical Spills*, "Community Members' Role in EPCRA—Discussion." www. chemicalspill.org.
7. "No Accident! How Industry and Government Agencies Are Failing to Prevent Chemical Spills," Communities for a Better Environment—California and Contra Costa Building and Construction Trades Council, p. 13.
8. Quoted in "Condea Vista Punished Over Leaks," *Chemistry and Industry,* November 3, 1997, p. 855.
9. Daniel Machalaba, "Local Ties: Decades of Mishandling Hazardous Cargo Leave Railroads a Toxic Legacy," *Wall Street Journal,* February 3, 1999, p. 1.

10. Glen Martin, "Ten Years Later Upper Sacramento River Alive After Deadly Pesticide Spill," *San Francisco Chronicle,* July 9, 2001.

Chapter 3: The Spills of War

11. Quoted in Mike Ahlers, "Report Cites Chemical Plants as Attractive Targets for Terrorists," *CNN.com*, March 19, 2003. www.cnn.com.

12. *Petroleum Economist*, "The Oil Fires Story," April 1992, p. 21.

13. Beth Daley, "Baghdad's Dark Skies Divide Health Specialists," *Boston Globe,* March 27, 2003, p. A29.

14. *Department of Veterans Affairs*, Health Benefits and Services, Gulf War Illness, Environment, "Frequently Asked Questions." www.va.gov.

15. Lee Gruzen, personal interview, April 17, 2003.

16. Gruzen, interview.

17. Gruzen, interview.

18. Gruzen, interview.

19. Gruzen, interview.

20. Quoted in Laurie Garrett, "Ill Winds of 9/11: Little Scrutiny for Brooklyn—Where Attack's Toxic Smoke Drifted," *Newsday*, August 23, 2002, p. 2D.

21. *New York Committee for Occupational Health and Safety*, NYCOSH Update on Safety and Health Archive, "Rep. Nadler, NYCOSH and Unions Demand EPA Cleanup of Lower Manhattan Workplaces," February 18, 2003. www.nycosh.org.

22. Quoted in "French Tanker Explosion Confirmed as Terror Attack," *International Policy Institute for Counter-Terrorism*, October 10, 2002. www.ict.org.il.

23. Tapper, "America's Achilles' Heel," *Salon.com.*

24. "Homeland Security: Voluntary Initiatives Are Underway at Chemical Facilities, But the Extent of Security Preparedness Is Unknown," General Accounting Office, GAO-03-439, March 2003, p. 1.

25. Quoted in Laura Meckler, "Terror Risk Cited for Common Industrial Chemicals," *Boston Globe*, April 9, 2003, p. 3A.

Chapter 4: Response and Cleanup

26. *Tasmanian Conservation Trust*, "Penguin Conservation in Tasmania." www.tct.org.au.

27. *Access Indiana*, Indiana Department of Environmental Management, 2002 State of the Environment Report, Land Quality, "Contaminated Sites." www.in.gov.

28. Sandy Smith, "Explosion Rocks N.C. Factory, Kills at Least Three Workers, Injures Dozens More," *Occupational Hazards*. www.occupationalhazards.com.

29. Christopher Bockman, "Mystery and Pain Go on for Toulouse," *BBC News*, October, 22, 2001. http://news.bbc.co.uk.

30. *Occupational Health and Safety Centre*, Publications, "Manual for Emergency First Aid and Antidote Treatment of Chemical Injuries in the Industrial Setting." www.ohscmumbai.org.

31. *National Oceanic and Atmospheric Administration*, "ALOHA." http://response.restoration.noaa.gov.

32. *Emergency Planning for Chemical Spills*, Off-Site Consequence Analysis, Modeling Spills, "Aloha." www.chemicalspill.org.

33. B. Magnus Francis, *Toxic Substances in the Environment*. New York: John Wiley & Sons, 1994, p. 296.

Chapter 5: Preventing Oil and Chemical Accidents

34. *U.S. PIRG*, "Protecting Communities from Chemical Hazards: Inherent Safety at Work." www.pirg.org.

35. Quoted in Paulo Prada, "EU Presses for Tanker Rules After Spill," *Boston Globe*, November 21, 2002, p. A36.

36. *World Wildlife Fund*, "Key Points of the Single-Hull vs Double-Hull Ships Issue," November 2002. www.panda.org.

37. *Oil Companies International Marine Forum*, News, "Double Hulled Tankers—Are They the Answer?" www.ocimf.com.

38. *National Environmental Law Center,* "Resolved Cases." www.nelconline.org.

39. Machalaba, "Local Ties," *Wall Street Journal.*

40. Quoted in Machalaba, "Local Ties," *Wall Street Journal.*

41. *Europa,* European Commission, "Workshop on Illicit Discharges, 26 November, 2001." http://intelligence. jrc.cec.eu.int.

42. Quoted in Erica Rolfe, "Envisat's ASAR Reveals Extent of Massive Oil Spill off Spanish Coast," *SpaceHike.com.* www.spacehike.com.

Glossary

acute effects: Rapid, short-term impact of spills associated with high concentrations of poisons.

bio-accumulation: Gathering and reconcentration of dispersed toxic substances into the cells of living organisms, where they often are passed up the food chain by predators, gaining in potency as organisms eat one another.

biodegradation: The biological consumption or breakdown of oil by small organisms that feed on it and digest its toxins, thus making the oil less harmful.

blowout: A high-pressure, frequently explosive, burst of gases, oil, or chemicals, often associated with underground wells, pipes, or pipelines.

carcinogen: A cancer-causing substance that stimulates cells to grow uncontrollably into tumors; these can destroy organs and may spread (metastasize) throughout the body, causing death if not stopped.

chronic effects: Long-term, often very slow impacts of spills associated with lower concentrations of poisons dispersed into the environment, often accumulated in organisms and passed up through the food chain and reconcentrated.

containment: Process of halting dispersal of oil or a chemical after a spill, thus allowing various methods of cleanup.

corrosive: A chemical process of burning (oxidation) that can be rapid, as in a strong chemical burning through metal, or slow as in rust eating through storage tanks.

dispersal: Process of spreading out and dilution of spills, often reducing acute deadliness of toxins, yet making them harder to gather and dispose of safely.

DNA (deoxyribonucleic acid): Substances in all cells that dictate how cells perform and reproduce; DNA damaged by poisons can cause errors that can lead to birth defects, illnesses, and cancer.

emulsion: Close cousin of mousse, except oil-in-water emulsions sink, carrying toxins into the water's depths and poisoning organisms residing at various levels.

food chain: The path of predators feeding on each other, usually beginning with the smallest microorganisms; toxins stored in cells are passed upward in greater concentrations to larger predators.

groundwater: Underground pools of water trapped in rock formations and absorbed into sandy soils like massive underground sponges.

hormone: Any of a number of substances produced in the body that stimulate essential functions, such as reproduction, metabolism (burning food for energy), and growth; chemicals that mimic hormones may cause malfunctions of these processes by altering normal, natural dosages.

mitigation: A step or strategy that limits or reduces the effects of a spill.

mousse: Water that has mixed with oil into a floating, foam-like state that lingers for long periods, sometimes years, carrying toxins long distances.

plume: A form of oil or chemical dispersal moved by wind, water, gravity, or air from a fixed point (a concentrated spill), whether aboveground or below, into a widening cone away from the force moving it.

reactive: The process of two or more chemicals, one usually a metal, mixing to form new chemical variations, sometimes explosively, sometimes turning harmless chemicals, when separate, into dangerous combinations that give off lethal gases or great heat.

remediation: Any means for halting, cleaning, or reducing the effects of a spill.

tarballs: Clumps of oil broken up by weathering that form sticky masses ranging in size from specks to coins to pancakes.

volatile: Capable of evaporating rapidly and creating a vapor that may be explosive or highly poisonous; the vapor may form dangerous clouds that can quickly be moved by winds.

weathering: Chemical and physical changes in oil caused by wind, rain, sunlight, and currents that break an oil slick into particles that form mousse, tarballs, emulsion, and troublesome variations that disperse into the environment.

For Further Reading

Books

Michael Allaby, *The Environment: How It Works.* London: Horus Editions, 1996. Useful introduction to life cycles, ecosystems, oceans, and soils.

Ellen Doris, *Marine Biology.* New York: Thames Hudson, 1993. Well-illustrated introduction to ocean life.

Charyn Jones, ed., *Chemistry.* New York: DK, 1993. Richly illustrated introduction and guide to chemical processes and reactions.

Christopher Lampton, *Chemical Accident.* Brookfield, CT: Millbrook Press, 1994. A handy primer about what chemicals are, the industry, and disasters.

Laurence Pringle, *Oil Spills: Damage, Recovery, and Prevention.* New York: William Morrow, 1993. Informative introduction to oil spills.

Stephen Zipko, *Toxic Threat: How Hazardous Substances Threaten Our Lives.* Englewood Cliffs, NJ: Prentice Hall, 1990. Strong focus on types of hazards and chemicals, including pesticides and herbicides.

Periodicals

Environmental Protection Agency, "Understanding Oil Spills and Oil Spill Response," Emergency Response Division, Publication 9200.5-105, July 1993.

John G. Mitchell, "In the Wake of the Spill: Ten Years After Exxon Valdez," *National Geographic*, March 1999.

National Oceanic and Atmospheric Administration, "Oil Spill Case Histories, 1967–1991: Summaries of Significant U.S. and International Spills," Hazardous Materials Response and Assessment Division, Report No. HMRAD 92-11, September 1992.

Websites

Chemical Safety and Hazard Investigation Board (www.chemsafety.gov). Offers useful background information and maintains the chemical incidents reports center.

Environmental Protection Agency (www.epa.gov). Provides general principles and links to information and regulations on oil.

National Transportation Safety Board (www.ntsb.gov). Useful background on marine and pipeline accidents.

Works Consulted

Books

Lorris Cokerham and Barbara Shane, eds., *Basic Environmental Toxicology.* Boca Raton, FL: CRC Press, 1994. Collected articles, quite technical, on major environmental hazards.

Theo Colborn, Dianne Dumanoski, and John Peterson Myers, *Our Stolen Future.* New York: Dutton, 1996. Highly readable scientific analysis about hormonal effects of toxic poisons moving through the food chain.

William M. Evan and Mark Manion, *Minding the Machines: Preventing Technological Disasters.* New York: Prentice Hall, 2002. A penetrating look at common factors in major accidents, from the *Titanic* to Bhopal.

B. Magnus Francis, *Toxic Substances in the Environment.* New York: John Wiley & Sons, 1994. Reliable information on many substances and chemicals.

Dominique Lapierre and Javier Moro, *Five Past Midnight in Bhopal.* New York: Warner Books, 2002. A gripping retelling of the Bhopal disaster.

Helmut F. Van Emden and David B. Peakall, *Beyond Silent Spring.* London: Chapman and Hall, 1996. A UN book about chemical safety and toxic hazards in the environment.

Periodicals

Chemistry and Industry, "Condea Vista Punished Over Leaks," November 3, 1997.

Beth Daley, "Baghdad's Dark Skies Divide Health Specialists," *Boston Globe,* March 27, 2003.

"Ecological Study of the Amoco Cadiz Oil Spill," National Oceanic and Atmospheric Administration, U.S. Government Printing Office, 1982.

Laurie Garrett, "Ill Winds of 9/11: Little Scrutiny for Brooklyn—Where Attack's Toxic Smoke Drifted," *Newsday*, August 23, 2002.

Louis J. Guillette Jr., et al., "Developmental Abnormalities of the Gonad and Abnormal Sex Hormone Concentrations in Juvenile Alligators from Contaminated and Control Lakes in Florida," *Environmental Health Perspectives*, vol. 102, no. 8, 1996.

"Homeland Security: Voluntary Initiatives Are Underway at Chemical Facilities, But the Extent of Security Preparedness Is Unknown," General Accounting Office, GAO-03-439, March 2003.

Daniel Machalaba, "Local Ties: Decades of Mishandling Hazardous Cargo Leave Railroads a Toxic Legacy," *Wall Street Journal*, February 3, 1999.

Glen Martin, "Ten Years Later Upper Sacramento River Alive After Deadly Pesticide Spill," *San Francisco Chronicle*, July 9, 2001.

Laura Meckler, "Terror Risk Cited for Common Industrial Chemicals," *Boston Globe*, April 9, 2003.

"No Accident! How Industry and Government Agencies Are Failing to Prevent Chemical Spills," Communities for a Better Environment—California and Contra Costa Building and Construction Trades Council.

Petroleum Economist, "The Oil Fires Story," April 1992.

Paulo Prada, "EU Presses for Tanker Rules After Spill," *Boston Globe*, November 21, 2002.

Internet Sources

Access Indiana, Indiana Department of Environmental Management, 2002 State of the Environment Report, Land Quality, "Contaminated Sites." www.in.gov.

Mike Ahlers, "Report Cites Chemical Plants as Attractive Targets for Terrorists," *CNN.com*, March 19, 2003. www.cnn.com.

Christopher Bockman, "Mystery and Pain Go on for Toulouse," *BBC News*, October, 22, 2001. http://news.bbc.co.uk.

Centers for Disease Control, "Occupational Health Guidelines for Chemical Hazards." www.cdc.gov.

Richard Charter, "The Renewable Roadmap to Energy Independence: Prepared Statement, Field Hearing of the Subcommittee on Energy," February 21, 2002, *The Democratic Caucus Committee on Science.* www.house.gov.

Department of Veterans Affairs, Health Benefits and Services, Gulf War Illness, Environment, "Frequently Asked Questions." www.va.gov.

Emergency Planning for Chemical Spills, "Community Members' Role in EPCRA—Discussion." www.chemicalspill.org.

————Off-Site Consequence Analysis, Modeling Spills, "Aloha." www.chemicalspill.org.

Europa, European Commission, "Workshop on Illicit Discharges, 26 November 2001." http://intelligence.jrc.cec.eu.int.

FEMA.gov, "Are You Ready? A Guide to Citizen Preparedness." www.fema.gov.

Greenpeace, "The Bhopal Disaster." www.greenpeace.org.

International Policy Institute for Counter-Terrorism, "French Tanker Explosion Confirmed as Terror Attack," October 10, 2002. www.ict.org.il.

National Environmental Law Center, "Resolved Cases." www.nelconline.org.

National Oceanic and Atmospheric Administration, "ALOHA." http://response.restoration.noaa.gov.

New York Committee for Occupational Safety and Health, "Rep. Nadler, NYCOSH and Unions Demand EPA Cleanup of Lower Manhattan Workplaces," February 18, 2003. www.nycosh.org.

Occupational Health and Safety Centre, Publications, "Manual for Emergency First Aid and Antidote Treatment of Chemical Injuries in the Industrial Setting." www.ohscmumbai.org.

Oil Companies International Marine Forum, News, "Double Hulled Tankers—Are They the Answer?" www.ocimf.com.

Red Adair, "The Fires of Kuwait." www.redadair.com.

Cynthia Ramos, "Gulf War Risk Factor Report Reprints," *Department of Veterans Affairs.* www.va.gov.

Erica Rolfe, "Envisat's ASAR Reveals Extent of Massive Oil Spill off Spanish Coast," *SpaceHike.com.* www.spacehike.com.

Yereth Rosen, "Exxon Valdez Oil Still Harmful, U.S. Studies Say," *Environmental News Network,* January 15, 2003. www.enn.com.

Sandy Smith, "Explosion Rocks N.C. Factory, Kills at Least Three Workers, Injures Dozens More," *Occupational Hazards.* www.occupationalhazards.com.

Jake Tapper, "America's Achilles' Heel," *Salon.com,* March 18, 2003. www.salon.com.

Tasmanian Conservation Trust, "Penguin Conservation in Tasmania." www.tct.org.au.

U.S. Environmental Protection Agency, Oil Program, "Ashland Oil Spill," www.epa.gov.

U.S. PIRG, "Protecting Communities from Chemical Hazards: Inherent Safety at Work." www.pirg.org.

World Wildlife Fund, "Key Points of the Single-Hull vs Double-Hull Ships Issue," November 2002. www.panda.org.

Websites

Air and Waste Management Association (www.awma.org). A nonprofit educational web resource.

International Tanker Owners Pollution Federation (www.itopf.com). Provides charts, graphs, and summary text on world shipping spills over several decades.

National Response Center (www.nrc.uscg.mil). The federal point of contact for reporting oil and chemical spills offers useful statistics, incident summaries, and links.

Emergency Planning for Chemical Spills (www.chemicalspill.org). Large public resource about planning and spill emergencies cast toward citizen groups and families.

Index

Picture Credits

About the Author

Peter Owens is an award-winning, widely published journalist, software author, web publisher, fiction writer, and educator. Two of his software packages, *The Research Paper Writer* and *The Classroom Newspaper Workshop,* were Tom Snyder Productions best-sellers. He founded *KidNews.com,* which won dozens of national awards and accolades. Owens earned his master's and doctoral degrees from Harvard University and was the Teacher of the Year at the University of Massachusetts Dartmouth, where he teaches professional writing. He lives on Cape Cod, Massachusetts.